BOSSHARDT

OMF International was founded by James Hudson Taylor in 1865 as the China Inland Mission. It now works in countries right along the Asia Pacific Rim. While evangelism and church planting are the Fellowship's central thrust, it also finds placements for Christian professionals with a wide range of expertise.

Bosshardt
A Biography

JEAN WATSON

OMF International

MONARCH
Crowborough

First published 1995

British Library Cataloguing Data
A catalogue record for this book is available
from the British Library.

ISBN 1 85424 297 0

Designed and produced by
Bookprint Creative Services
P.O. Box 827, BN21 3YJ, England for
MONARCH PUBLICATIONS
Broadway House, The Broadway,
Crowborough, E. Sussex, TN6 1HQ
Printed in Great Britain.

To my parents,
Bill and Lilian Simmonds

CONTENTS

THANKS AND ACKNOWLEDGMENTS

I gratefully acknowledge my indebtedness to Alfred Bosshardt's autobiographies: *The Restraining Hand,* the first account of his captivity (Hodder & Stoughton, 1936); and *The Guiding Hand,* covering more of his life as told to Edward England and his late first wife, Gwen (OMF, 1973, 1990). Very useful, too, have been: the manuscript of Arnolis Hayman's account of his captivity; a book called *The Long March — The Untold Story,* by Harrison Salisbury (Macmillan, 1985); a TV Channel 4 Programme, 1988 — 'Witness of the Long March'; Alfred's letters; and various articles, particularly some by Anthony Grey. Grey's novels, too, along with Jung Chang's *Wild Swans* (Flamingo, 1993), have been invaluable in terms of background and context; in this connection they also, helpfully if incidentally, reactivated some of my own memories of being in China for the first fifteen years of my life.

Many people shared with me their memories of Alfred or read and commented on the manuscript, particularly David Brunnschweiler, Marilyn Luck, Bernard and Jean Welch, Sau Wai Wong, Chee Yan Chow, Douglas and Rosie Sadler, Judith Gabler, John and Margaret Hodgkinson, Beatrice Jackson, Brenda and Deryck Thompson, Chor Hin Ong, Henry Ly, Albert Pope, Patrick and Ursula Grace, Irma Piaget, Edith Sutcliffe, Bill Simmonds, Annie Lee, Eve Killey, Elizabeth Archibald, David and Margaret Killingray, and various members of OMF International.

To everyone, named or not, who contributed information, inspiration and help — my very warm thanks.

Finally, a note about verses and names: I have left Bible verses in the version or words in which Alfred quoted or remembered them, but used modern spelling for most Chinese names, both for places and people – putting surnames first or last according to whether the people concerned were or are living in China or the West.

AUTHOR'S PREFACE

'I hear you're writing a book about my Mr Bosshardt,' she said.

The speaker was one of the devoted team of nurses and carers who look after retired missionaries in Cornford House, Pembury, Kent.

'That's right,' I replied.

'He was a lovely man,' she reminisced warmly. 'He told us that his wife was buried in another country and that the Chinese there still looked after her grave. It made him really happy to think that after all those years they still did that... And another time he told us that his enemy had become his friend: he was so excited and happy about that as well... Oh, and something that made him laugh was that the doctor who saw him after he was released said that what he'd been through would take ten years off his life! He thought that was very funny – because there he was in his nineties... He really was a lovely man...'

I was moved by her words and fell to thinking of Alfred Bosshardt at that time: elderly and frail, severely paralysed and almost totally dependent on others – yet still joyful. Why? Because, twenty-five years on, his beloved wife's grave was being lovingly tended by the people they'd lived amongst; and because his enemy had become his friend. And still having a quiet chuckle about confounding the experts and outliving his predicted earlier demise.

He died at the age of ninety-six. During his last three years at Cornford house his bed-sitting-room was next to my mother's, so I often saw him in passing.

After working for seventy years among the Chinese in three

different countries, his world had been reduced to that one room. But only through physical weakness and incapacity; his mind remained as clear and alert as ever. If he wasn't praying, dictating or reading, he was talking and laughing with his many visitors – family and friends, people from the media and other contacts.

What was it, I used to wonder, that drew such a variety of people to him from all round the world?

I knew he had taken part in the Long March across China by the Red Army in the mid-1930s. But not until I was preparing to write his biography, a year after his death, did I begin to appreciate the full story and, more importantly, the quality and essence of the person who was Alfred Bosshardt. His truly mind-blowing experiences and achievements rightly earned him a unique place in the history of missionary work in China. But it was his spirit and character that so greatly endeared him to the Chinese people and to so many others during the course of his long life.

I have written the book for all the thousands of people whose lives Alfred and Rose have already touched, and for future generations looking for real heroes and saints as role models and sources of inspiration. Anthony Grey, victim of the Cultural Revolution of the 1960s, referred to Alfred as 'perhaps the most saintly individual I have ever met' (*The Daily Telegraph* Obituaries, 6.11.93). Others have expressed similar opinions. And I'm sure they all had in mind genuine saintliness, not its unattractive, sanctimonious counterfeit.

Alfred's goodness was both real and warm. He was other-worldly and down-to-earth; a saint with a Mancunian accent and a great sense of humour, who crocheted socks to keep the feet of his captors warm in the bitter Chinese winter. In writing his biography, I had no need to embellish or gloss over reality, even if I had wanted to. The man and his story are sufficiently luminous and winsome in their own right.

At least they are for me. You must judge for yourself, and I invite you to do so.

THE ROAD TAKEN – OCTOBER 1934

A little party of travellers faces a choice of roads.

Alfred and Rose Bosshardt have been working in inland China as missionaries for over ten years. For the past three, since their marriage, they have lived and worked in Zhenyuan, Guizhou province. Some days ago they left home to join colleagues for a time of prayer. Now they are eager to get back home and continue their work with fresh energy and enthusiasm. Accompanying them are six Chinese people.

Which road should they take? Bandits are an ever-present threat and there have been rumours of fighting, so they think it best to choose the route which is likely to be better protected by government troops – the newer, shorter road.

They proceed along this to the village where they plan to spend the night. When they are nearly there, ascending the last hill, armed men erupt from the bushes and take them captive.

Abruptly husband and wife are torn apart and Alfred is catapulted into an existence fraught with extremes of physical and emotional hardship, in which justice is savagely rough and punishment brutal, and untimely death and other horrors are never far away. How long it will last or what will be its outcome, they have no idea.

Why did the travellers take the road which led to all that? Was it bad luck or human error that caused them to walk into an ambush that day?

Alfred and Rose were never in any doubt as to how to answer such questions. Despite all that happened, for the rest of their lives they steadily maintained, 'We both felt that the choice lay in God's hands.'

Such faith has long, deep roots.

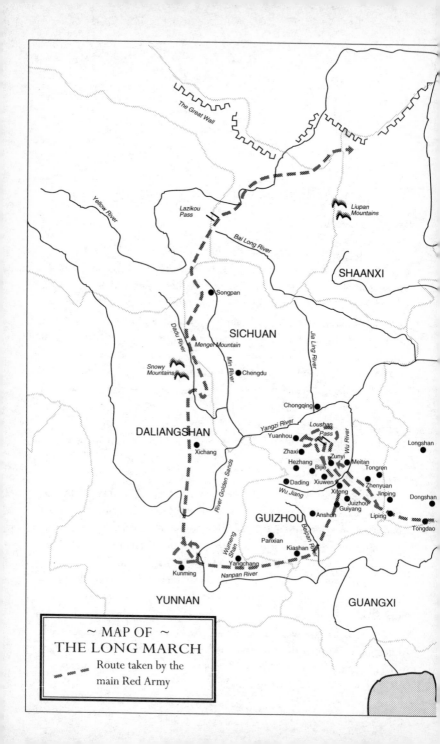

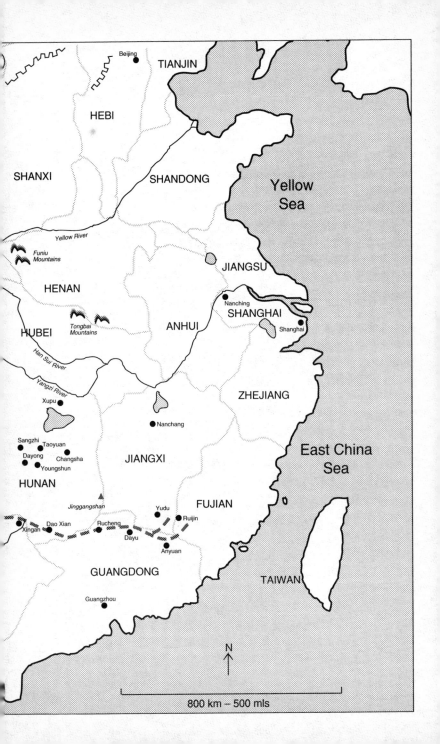

MANCHESTER AND LONDON
1897-1922

EARLY CALL

A crowded Baptist Church in Moss Side Manchester in 1906. On the platform, the dynamic figure of Charles Fairclough, a missionary from inland China on home leave. After ten years there, he speaks fluent Chinese with a trace of his native Lancashire accent. Now, speaking in English similarly accented, he is giving an enthusiastic account of the work of the missionary society to which he belongs, the China Inland Mission.

He says that when the CIM began in 1865 there were fifteen Protestant mission stations in China, claiming about 2,000 converts between them. By 1906, through the CIM alone, more than 14,000 people have become converts to the Christian faith. Staffed by nearly 850 missionaries with over 1,000 Chinese helpers, the mission is responsible for about 450 churches and 150 schools, as well as forty hospitals or dispensaries and one hundred opium refuges.

Not the stuff, on the face of it, to hold the interest of a boy of ten. But Charles Fairclough's enthusiasm for God and China is infectious. He conveys information and then challenges his listeners about the millions as yet ignorant of the Christian message. Who will go to them with that message? Any who choose to do so will not find the task easy: eighty members of the mission, including twenty-two children, were murdered in one year during the Boxer massacre of foreigners, sanctioned by the Empress Dowager. Who will take their places?

As he sits in his pew, Alfred's whole being silently cries out, 'I will'. Charles Fairclough doesn't ask for money, but Alfred and his friends gladly give their all. If a tram car had turned up at that moment with China as its destination, they would gleefully have jumped aboard, trusting God to provide what was needed. For, as Alfred was to write later, 'The danger and adventure of a missionary's life conquered my imagination.'

He was to encounter plenty of both in the coming years. Meanwhile, he grew from boyhood to manhood in Manchester – the place to which his parents had come as young and single people from German-speaking areas of Switzerland. Heinrich Alfred Bosshardt, born in Winterthur, Zurich, and Marie Forster in Oberuzwil, St Gallen, had left their beautiful but impoverished homeland for the more prosperous and diversified economy of Britain.

Their choice of Manchester had not been surprising. It was at that time the first industrial city in the world, dominating much of north-western England. Famous for its highly successful textile industries, it was also one of the world's great engineering centres, an important market for a huge trade in chemicals, and the heart of a vast distribution system for food, clothing and building materials. People had long been arriving from all over Europe and elsewhere to live and work there, and benefit from its education system and cultural life.

Heinrich and Marie had met at a Manchester cotton mill, where he was making patent drawings of spinning machinery and she was teaching the new technique of embroidering by machine. Their marriage had taken place in Switzerland in 1889, but afterwards the couple had returned to set up house in Moss Side, then a pleasant inner city suburb. Heinrich was never to return to Switzerland and Marie only once, and English was to be the language spoken in their home.

Their son, Rudolf Alfred, always called by his second name, was born on January 1st in the year of Queen Victoria's Diamond Jubilee, 1897. By then his older sisters, Ida and Frieda, were aged seven and three. A year later his third sister, Lily, was born.

There was also 'brother' Charlie, who was in fact a cousin, the son of one of Marie's sisters. When Charlie's young mother had died of TB, his aunt had adopted him. But at the age of nineteen, when Alfred was seven, Charlie emigrated to Canada and it was to be many years before they met up again.

Much loved himself, Alfred responded lovingly to others. Essentially serious and responsible, he also had a great sense of fun and a zest for life. A certain natural shyness was balanced by his liking for people; and his modesty was offset by his qualities of enthusiasm, loyalty and determination. At school he showed ability in the more practical subjects. Music, a traditional aspect of life in Lancashire, was one of his great loves. He played the piano and had a good singing voice which he put to good use by joining the church and school choirs.

His home was a happy place. Marie and Heinrich were gentle, gracious people. Though far from affluent, they were contented, indeed grateful, to have work which brought in enough money to meet their family's needs. The wealth generated by the city's booming industries was unevenly distributed. And the Bosshardt family were well aware of Manchester's poorer streets and houses, where many lived in want and squalor.

When Alfred was four, his parents became committed Christians and began attending Moss Side Baptist Church, taking their family with them. His own personal decision to become a Christian was made when he was nine, and he was baptised, as a public confirmation of his commitment, eight years later.

For him, church was not a boring experience. Under the preaching of Arnold Streuli, the lively, outgoing congregation began to experience revival, and numbers attending services rose from 200 to 800.

One result was greater interest in mission at home and abroad. Alfred had not forgotten the meeting at which he believed God had called him to China. Rather, the memory had remained vivid, spurring him on to find out more and get more involved. By the age of sixteen he was giving reports on China to the young people's meetings. He also collected money for missionaries. But the methods he used began to change as he learnt of the CIM's 'faith' principle. This had been spelt out by the mission's founder, Hudson Taylor – a northerner like Alfred, but from Barnsley, Yorkshire.

Instead of asking people for money, Hudson Taylor had prayed that God would supply all his needs in his own time and way; and it had been his lifelong experience that God had done exactly that. This principle had been incorporated into the mission he had founded. Its members made no direct appeals for money. Instead, they prayed that God would move people to contribute whatever it was right for them to give and for the mission to receive, so that the work he had in mind, and that alone, could be done.

Much struck by this, Alfred gave up canvassing and focused on prayer. He lost a few reluctant donors but the total missionary giving went up. He and four others agreed to support and pray for a Korean theological student in Seoul.

He also started to meet with friends from local churches to pray for China. This weekly meeting in his home was to be amazingly enduring and effective. An early outcome was the holding of open-air services opposite the local cinema. For, as they agreed one evening, concern for China 7,000 miles away didn't absolve them from fulfilling their responsibilities towards those closer at hand.

After a new pastor came to Moss Side Baptist Church, Alfred and others decided to join Union Hall Evangelical Church, led and pastored by Francis Thompson. Alfred was to have close, lifelong links with this church, which was to become outstanding for sending out missionaries and giving them practical and loving support.

Increasingly, Hudson Taylor's principles and life focused and sharpened Alfred's sense of call and his vision. The man had·died in 1905, when Alfred was eight, but his words and work lived on, through the mission and through the pages of Howard and Geraldine Taylor's biographies. Hudson's burden for a million Chinese a month dying without the gospel; his prayer for twenty-four evangelists for inland China; the account he opened for the China Inland Mission with a £10 deposit; his adoption of Chinese dress, culture and language: all this was eagerly absorbed and reflected on by the young man.

At seventeen, Alfred left school. His practical abilities seemed best suited to an apprenticeship in engineering. In the year that he began this training, the First World War broke out. He offered himself for service in the medical corps but was turned down because of his German name. This upset him at the time. Later, confronted by the realities of war, he decided that, if necessary, he would have been prepared to serve in the Red Cross but not to fight. And, for half a day a week, he helped at a Red Cross hospital.

At twenty-one, when the war ended, he had to choose between British and Swiss nationality. Unlike the rest of the family, he opted for the latter. The short-term consequence of this was that he was not called up for military service. Long-term, his decision would prove to be something of a lifeline.

Ida was now a pastry-cook and Frieda a schoolteacher. Lily was working for the Faith Mission in Edinburgh and Alfred was only waiting to complete his engineering training before applying to the China Inland Mission.

At a human level he was very diffident about his chances of being accepted: 'My talents were commonplace. Was there a place for ordinary people as missionaries?' Most of the missionaries he admired seemed to be very gifted people, with a university education behind them. He didn't see himself in their league, and would often say, 'I have the hands of an apprentice rather than the mind of a student.' But if God wanted him to go as a missionary to China – he would supply his needs and make him adequate for the task. On that point Alfred felt no ambivalence.

He was invited to attend the CIM conference at Swanwick, among the hills and dales of Derbyshire. While he was there, he met and talked with members of the CIM Council. They offered him three months' training in London, with no guarantee of acceptance at the end of it. It would mean giving up his job at a time when work was scarce and ex-servicemen were swelling the numbers queuing up outside Manchester's labour exchanges.

But, at twenty-three, Alfred decided to take this, his first step of faith.

PREPARATION

Alfred waved goodbye to family and friends at the station in Manchester and boarded the train for London. On arriving at St Pancras he collected his bicycle, sent on by rail in advance, and cycled along in the wake of a No 73 bus which he knew would be passing close to his destination.

Arriving safely at the mission's headquarters in Newington Green, north London, he dismounted and paused to survey the large building. The text inscribed in stone over its main doorway filled him with a mixture of awe and excitement. 'Have faith in God': words which had inspired all the 'great' missionaries of the past who had come to this place were now addressed to him!

The next three months would bring his thirteen-year-old dream one step closer to realisation. But only if, having watched the way he lived and related to others, the mission chiefs decided he was suitable for further training. To Alfred's delighted relief, they did. 'Whatever my failings,' he wrote, 'the Council decided that I should remain for the full two years' Biblical and practical training.'

There were women as well as men on the course, but romantic involvements were strongly discouraged. In any case, lack of time and strict segregation of the sexes gave them little chance to develop.

Theology, including a thorough grasp of the Bible and the Christian faith was obviously crucial. The prospective missionaries needed to be very clear about the Christian message, not least because it would undoubtedly clash with China's prevalent polytheism, in which animism and ancestor worship, overlaid by

Taoism, Confucianism and Buddhism, were closely bound up with sorcery and magic.

Learning about Chinese religions and ideologies formed part of a very necessary course of studies on China's country and people, its history and society, its culture and language. In marked contrast to Britain, the patterns and structures of life in China for ordinary people had remained largely unchanged for hundreds of years. Most of the Chinese people were still landless peasants making a precarious living from the soil. Of the rest, there was a smaller group of merchants, artisans and craftsmen, and finally an élite band of landowners who controlled education and nearly all other walks of public and private life.

As part of their preparation for the country and its culture, Alfred and two other students visited London's Chinatown. Here they walked among Chinese people, bought some Chinese pens and ate a Chinese meal. It was as they were attempting to eat the steaming rice and quick-fried pork and vegetables with chopsticks that they had a taste, in more than one sense, of things to come. For there they were, three lone Europeans, a tiny, vulnerable, foreign minority, surrounded and under scrutiny by a Chinese majority.

Along with theological and China studies, the students were taught advanced First Aid. In areas where hospitals and medical staff were few and far between, missionaries often came to the rescue. Even basic medical knowledge and skills could make the difference between life and death.

It was the task of Dr Tom Bragg to teach Alfred and his fellow-students the elements of diagnosis and treatment and train them in some necessary practical skills. 'Admirable!' he would say whenever he could truthfully do so. Alfred's later comment, reflecting his gentle tongue-in-cheek humour, was: 'There were days when he had terrible misgivings about us, as we tied ourselves in knots with bandages, and confidently prescribed the wrong remedies.'

Alfred threw himself into the hard work and fun of student life for two years. Then came the final crucial interview with the mission's council. He approached this with a typical mixture of personal diffidence and confidence in God.

'Have you any personal experience of God providing for your needs?' he was asked. After a moment's thought, he offered the fact that his fare for China, for which he'd saved up before coming to London, was still intact. He'd fully expected to have to dip into it during the two years' training. But it was surely God's provision that he hadn't had to do so.

The council listened and deliberated. Their following criteria were not based on educational or other personal qualifications:

'While thankful for any educational advantages that candidates may have enjoyed, we attach far greater importance to spiritual qualifications. We desire men* who believe that there is a God and that he is both intelligent and faithful, and who therefore trust him; who believe that he is the rewarder of those who diligently seek him, and are therefore men of prayer. We desire men who believe the Bible to be the word of God, and who accepting the declaration, "All power is given unto me," are prepared to carry out to the best of their ability the command, "Go … teach all nations," relying on him who possesses "all power" and has promised to be with his messengers "always".'

On this basis, the council informed Alfred and ten other relieved and delighted candidates that they had been accepted for missionary work in inland China.

Some 2,000 people gathered at Kingsway Hall in London for their farewell service. Alfred's mother was among them. There was a close bond between mother and son. She prayed for the strength to give Alfred wholeheartedly and fully to God for the work to which she believed he had been called. Her prayer was answered but not easily and not without pain. For China was the other

---

*'Men' in this context denoted women as well as men, since the China Inland Mission along with other missions – well ahead of their time in this respect – accepted women on the same grounds and for the same work as men.

side of the world and those who went there faced many dangers.

During the second half of the nineteenth century, vast numbers of people had flocked there from many different countries and for a whole variety of reasons. Missionaries wanting to share, however imperfectly, a message of God's love and forgiveness. Those in search of conquest, adventure or knowledge. Colonists hoping to obtain land and rights. People in business and commerce eager to offer their goods and services to 400 million potential customers, or to take advantage of the country's gold, jade, silk, tea and other products and natural resources.

To a proud people, long accustomed to thinking of themselves as the centre of the earth, the mere presence of strangers had felt like an intrusion.

Exploitation and the taking over of their key ports by some of these had added insult to injury. And all too often this had resulted in resentment and hostility towards all foreigners, regardless of whether they were honourable and caring or greedy and self-seeking.

At the same time, China had other problems. It had been ruled since the mid-seventeenth century by the weak, corrupt and oppressive Manchu empire. This had been overthrown in 1911. But the republic under Sun Yat-sen had then not been able to establish itself, so the country had been plunged into political chaos and civil war.

Military governors of provinces fought one another to gain more land and power, and central government was powerless to stop them. Powerful warlords emerged and, in many cases, ruled by terror and oppression. There was often little to distinguish their soldiers from the robber bands which roamed the countryside and engaged in extortion, looting and pillage.

Alfred knew that this was the situation within which he was going to have to work. But, along with most other people, he was not aware of the strength of the socialist feeling in the country, which had led to the founding, in 1921, of the Chinese Communist Party.

And he certainly had no inkling that he would get caught up in events which, in decisively shaping Chinese Communism, would affect every aspect of the country's life, not least the Christian church and missionary work there.

CHINA – 1922-1934

NEW WORLD

Nothing could have prepared Alfred for the variety and exuberance of life all around him.

It was November and he was walking through the streets of the vast walled city of Shanghai, the greatest of China's foreign treaty ports on the river Huangpu fifteen miles from the Yangzi estuary. He and the other new missionaries had five days in which to start adjusting to a whole new way of life before moving on to the language school.

Many different nationalities thronged the crowded water-front, roads and alleyways of the metropolis. But inevitably the four million Chinese were predominant – wave upon wave of blue-gowned figures, their black hair held in place by colourful bandanas, hidden under white turbans or protruding from large circular yellow hats, their feet bare or shod in straw sandals.

Everywhere, people were publicly getting on with their lives. Exchanging greetings or plying their wares, shouting to one another or passers-by, their voices ranging rapidly up and down a register of higher and lower tones. Cooking, eating, begging, spitting, coughing. Pursuing their trades as bootblacks, scribes, jewellers, porters...

In a country full of contrasts, Shanghai seemed to epitomise the gulf between the rich in their silks and satins, with their servants and personal transport, and the poor, living in gutters or hovels in conditions of unimaginable want and squalor.

The journey from London by boat, docking at Marseilles, Singapore and Hongkong, had taken nearly six weeks. On arrival,

Alfred had looked eagerly for letters from home. There had been none. But, keeping his disappointment and anxiety considerately in check, he had written: 'There were no home letters awaiting me on arrival, but ... they will be all the sweeter when they arrive. This letter must bring you my Christmas greetings. It will be the first time we have not been a complete family for the occasion. Yet, but for the first Christmas, I would not be here.'

The mission station from which he had sent this letter was a haven of peace in the midst of the thronging, noisy city. Here older, experienced missionaries were on hand to help and talk to the new recruits. Among others, D. E. Hoste, the Director who had succeeded Hudson Taylor, offered them wise, memorable advice: 'Take care that nothing you say or do creates barriers between yourselves as missionaries and the Chinese people. Remember you come to China as servants, following the example of Jesus.'

They shopped for vital necessities – bedding, an oil sheet, a mat, a basket, a Chinese-English dictionary, a Chinese New Testament, some primers and other books for language study. But they found that being treated as objects of great curiosity, and not being able to understand a word of the excited chattering going on all around them, slowed them down considerably and was most disconcerting.

Soon they travelled to Zhenjiang. The walk from the railway station to the language school was impeded by beggars, pedlars and rickshaw owners, out for money or custom and prepared to be very resourceful and persistent in getting them.

Later Alfred was to realise that some of the beggars were 'professional' – able-bodied people who made begging a way of life if not an art form, faking injuries and fabricating hard-luck stories. But there was still a distressing number of genuinely disabled and destitute people on every hand.

Samuel and Janet Glanville were in charge of the language school. Alfred was delighted to discover that Janet had trained in Manchester twenty years earlier.

The students adopted Chinese dress – dark blue wadded gowns

and straw sandals – and were given Chinese names by their teacher, Mr Liu. Traditionally chosen to reflect something of the character of the individual concerned, names had great significance in China. Alfred was to be known as Bo Sha-deo, meaning, 'Although thin and small, he has understanding and discernment.' The physical reference was rather surprising since he was taller and bigger-boned than the average Chinese man. Later, when he went to Guizhou, he was dubbed Bo Fu-li, meaning 'unselfish'.

Mr Liu taught spoken Chinese, while Samuel Glanville focused on the grammar. Alfred worked hard and with enthusiasm, but acquiring a new language proved quite a struggle for him.

At last the long-delayed letter from home arrived. He fell on it with anxious eagerness, and was relieved to learn that all was well. At the same time, hearing from loved ones while still trying to adjust to being separated from them was not an unmixed joy. For, as he wrote, 'The disturbing of deep roots, however gently done, is very painful.'

But the stimulation and pressures of life in Zhenjiang left no time or energy for brooding, even if Alfred had been so inclined. The students were expected to give six hours a day to language study, rising at 6 a.m. and going to bed at 10 p.m. – a rigorous regime, on top of all the other adjustments. Alfred commented to his family, 'I get very tired and have overslept two or three times, so I will have to watch myself.'

Particularly trying was the constant noise. The boom of the gong from the Buddhist convent next door was perhaps the pleasantest in a cacophony of sounds which included the whining of beggars; the sharp cries of bamboo-clacking street vendors; the ringing of bells by blind children passing by; the shouts of barrowmen and rickshaw drivers needing to clear a gangway; the repetitive *heh hos* of teams of porters carrying laden sedan or mountain chairs at shoulder height.

Trying to learn a difficult tonal language against that background was enough to defeat all but the most dedicated.

Christmas came – Alfred's first away from his family. It was their loving, familiar presence that he missed – not the seasonal trappings. A tree, which he and fellow-students had found after an hour's walk and then carried back and decorated, gave their living room a sufficiently festive air. And there were cards from the Glanvilles and from the Director and his wife.

After their meal Samuel Glanville read out a verse which struck Alfred and remained in his memory – a promise from the book of Ruth: 'Thou hast left thy father and mother and the land of thy nativity and art come unto a people thou knewest not heretofore. The Lord recompense thy work and a full reward be given thee of the Lord God of Israel, under whose wings thou art come to trust.'

By the New Year, Alfred had managed to learn the Lord's Prayer in Chinese. But he could hardly recite this to the curious onlookers as he walked through the town's main street – no wider than a Manchester pavement, although the town's population was 300,000. On either side, houses and shops were open to view, their contents and occupants spilling out into the dirt road. Here, a dentist tugged vigorously at a client's tooth; there, a barber was deftly shaving faces, trimming hair and beards.

Again, beggars were everywhere and importunate. One had no feet and 'walked' with his hands. His head was shaved and there was a hole in his skull – perhaps self-inflicted – into which lighted incense sticks had been placed. In amongst the human population were hungry, homeless dogs, scavenging for scraps, along with rooting pigs and squawking chickens.

A street chapel provided a welcome respite from the surrounding chaos and confusion. Alfred joined the people there, quietly sitting and listening to the preacher speaking of eternal realities.

Winter gave way to spring and brought the arrival of the Director to assign the students to the mission stations and areas in which they were to work. Alfred felt at peace, convinced that this man would know where God wanted him to be.

Mr Hoste was seated at a table covered by a large map of China. After prayer, he pointed to the place which he had in mind for Alfred.

Zunyi, the second largest town in northern Guizhou, had a well-established church and the mission station was run by Peter and Lily Olesen. Some time earlier, these senior missionaries had been attacked by robbers while travelling. Though very scared and shaken, Lily was now willing to return with her husband to their mission station. Alfred readily agreed to join the couple.

To his disappointment, their journey was delayed. Peter Olesen was needed for overseeing some building work at the school for missionaries' children in Chefoo. While he went off to do this, Alfred went to Chongqing, in Sichuan province, to continue his language study.

Two weeks after his arrival, he received two telegrams from Manchester. One told him that his sister Frieda was gravely ill with TB; the other that she had died. She would have been thirty on her next birthday. While Alfred was struggling with his grief, a long-delayed letter arrived. It was from Frieda. Reading it after he had heard of her death was unbearably poignant.

While Alfred was in the hills for the summer, Chongqing was caught in a feud between two warlord generals. One of these, nicknamed 'the butcher', besieged the city for a week. The fighting continued into August. Alfred spent a night in the city just as another siege was beginning. Water supplies had been cut off and rice was very scarce. Shopkeepers not already cleaned out by soldiers or bandits, between which there was very little to choose, had barricaded their premises as best they could. People went in fear of their lives and public executions were not uncommon.

Alfred witnessed one of these. Two condemned men were paraded through the streets. Bound hand and foot and stripped to the waist, each wearing a placard proclaiming his crimes, they were taken to the execution ground. There, surrounded by jeering spectators, they were beheaded.

It was a relief to get out of the city and go to stay with colleagues, Herbert and Edith Curtis, at their mission station at Jiangjin further along the Yangzi river. Life here was more peaceful than in Chonqing, although some homes were looted and one day Alfred saw four dead soldiers lying in the street. News that ten thousand soldiers would be passing through the city, expecting to be fed, caused widespread alarm and some women asked to be allowed to sleep in the mission premises.

In this situation, Alfred had ample opportunity to gain greater fluency in the language and increase his understanding of the people and their culture.

Opposite his room was a Chinese school. He enjoyed seeing the children at play and listening to them shouting out their lessons, learning by rote and repetition.

Other experiences were far less pleasant. At the local prison the inmates were kept in overcrowded, insanitary conditions. The resulting stench and filth were indescribable, and in the midst of this were the pitiful captives with their emaciated bodies, hollow cheeks and huge, hopeless eyes. Alfred spoke to them and gave out leaflets, knowing that at best his visit would only be a slight, momentary diversion in the long, dark misery of their lives.

He also accompanied his colleagues as they visited shops and homes, to sell Chinese gospels and to invite people to the Sunday services at the chapel. These were usually attended by about fifty adults and eighty children.

Life was busy and Alfred was happy with the Curtises, but he longed to be at the station to which he'd been assigned. And at last he and Peter Olesen were on their way, escorted by thirty soldiers, leaving Lily and a colleague to follow at a later date when things were safer.

Before setting off Alfred wrote to his family:

'Whichever way we go, there will be danger. My New Year text is: "Say not, I am a child: for thou shalt go to all I send thee and whatsoever I command thee thou shalt speak." I am twenty-seven today. Truly I am getting an old man.'

The journey took them through a great many plundered villages. On top of this, the hilly terrain and rough roads made walking very difficult. Things were even worse for the porters, having to carry the luggage and feeling the butt end of the soldiers' rifles if ever they showed signs of flagging. The missionaries' protests about this treatment fell on deaf ears.

Peter and Alfred encouraged one another from the Psalms. 'I will both lay me down in peace, and sleep, for thou only makest me dwell in safety,' they read – reassured as much by the words as by the thought of all the people down the years who had held on to this promise and proved its truth. Alfred was buoyed up, too, by Peter's mature character and faith. With hindsight, he would see this journey as a faint foreshadowing of another one.

For the last leg, the missionaries and their escort attached themselves to a caravan of salt-carriers and their soldiers. The first day the enlarged party walked twenty-five miles along winding tracks, through spectacularly beautiful cliffs.

It was a hazardous trip during which one false step could have brought disaster. However they arrived, weary and footsore but safe, at a farmhouse where they bedded down for the night.

The next day they entered Guizhou, one of China's most undeveloped and sparsely populated provinces at that time. As well as the Chinese population, there was a great variety of tribal minorities with their own distinctive customs and culture, scattered throughout the region. Alfred was to get to know and love Guizhou, with its dramatic scenery of steep mountains and spectacular waterfalls, its moist, mild climate and lush and colourful vegetation. Most of all he would love its people.

Again the travellers slept in a farmhouse. There, tiredness forgotten in his immense joy at being now so close to Zunyi, Alfred wrote a letter to his former Moss Side Baptist Church pastor, Arnold Streuli.

The journey had taken them three weeks instead of ten days, but now it was over and they walked through the gates and into the city.

The Christians were out in force to welcome Peter Olesen.

Telling the story against himself and in humorous vein, Alfred was to write later:

'Suddenly I was left out. In their happiness at seeing him after a year's absence they forgot me – God's gift from Manchester! They had not been awaiting my arrival, but the older missionary's. Their forgetfulness was exactly long enough for God's whisper, then I was caught up in their celebrations. There *was* a place for me.'

NEW MISSIONARY

Alfred walked through the streets of Zunyi, northern Guizhou, in south-west China. Like most Chinese cities, it was surrounded by high walls and gates. He decided to take a stroll outside the gates, but was soon pulled up short at the sight of a violent scuffle which ended in a man's death.

Chinese New Year was about to be celebrated. As Alfred had just witnessed, feelings at such a time were likely to be volatile, not least because traditionally accounts were supposed to be settled in the run up to the festival. On hearing what had happened, Peter advised his new young colleague against venturing outside the city unaccompanied.

Alfred was given a couple of rooms in an attractive, well-constructed wooden house, built around two courtyards with their tubs of bright flowers. The property was owned by a rich Chinese family. After several daughters had been born to them, they deemed their home to be haunted; so they built and moved into another house next door. In this way, they hoped to win favour with their gods and so be granted the son for whom they so desperately longed and prayed. The mission benefited in that the family was willing to rent out at reasonable rates the premises they had vacated.

Alfred settled down to life with his first senior missionaries – Lily Olesen having joined her husband at Zunyi in the meantime. The Christian congregation there numbered about a hundred; of these seventy had been baptised as fully committed members. A month after his arrival, on his mother's birthday, Alfred preached his first sermon in Chinese, reading out the characters he had painstakingly copied and then rehearsed with his teacher. To his delight, his hearers understood what he was trying to tell them about the Good Shepherd.

His Chinese speaking was further stimulated when he found himself having to hold the fort during the Olesens' absence. This entailed accompanying the local Chinese evangelists on their visits to nearby villages, meeting the Christians there and helping to conduct services. Sometimes they arrived to find that bandits had been there before them. Then they would offer whatever comfort and practical help they could to the devastated, frightened survivors.

Alfred's own encounter with bandits was not long in coming. After robbing him and his fellow-traveller, the thieves left them tied to tree trunks. The two men managed to free themselves and walk to the next village. The head men there offered them twenty armed soldiers as an escort. Some merchants joined the group and they all set off, only to be raided by more bandits. This time the travellers were released after they had handed over the goods the merchants were carrying.

Back in Zunyi, Alfred learnt that he was to have new senior missionaries, the Robinsons. But their arrival was delayed, so he continued for a time to be the only European on the station. 'It seems to be my lot to be alone,' was his rather wistful comment. But the church deacon was sensitive to the missionary's situation, and invited him to his home for meals twice a day. This man, Mr Liu, was someone whom Alfred was increasingly to admire and respect.

Jack and Adeline Robinson finally arrived, with their two young boys, Peter and John. Having seen only Chinese people for so long, Alfred found the sight of Europeans quite a shock.

'You're so pale!' he exclaimed. The Robinsons laughed and reminded him that the same applied to him.

Not long afterwards famine struck the district. The cycle of devastation began when the rains came early, before the opium crops had been reaped or the rice crop sown. Deprived of rice sales, the country people tried to sell coal, but they had to drop the price drastically before anyone could afford to buy it. Rice porridge kitchens were opened.

Jack Robinson sent to Beijing asking for relief funds, but nothing happened. So, certain that God wanted them to get involved in helping the needy, he persuaded an official to lend him a redundant Buddhist temple in which he planned to give food and shelter to as many people as possible.

On the first day, twelve mothers came with their babies; on the next, about forty. With the arrival of twenty more, capacity was reached. The condition of the refugees was pitiful. Though half-starved themselves, the mothers were attempting to feed their hungry distressed babies.

Alfred and Jack had built a stove, but it did not give off enough heat to keep out the biting cold. There was makeshift bedding for the people to lie on, but no covering for them. A business man who heard about this sent some sacking along, and Alfred helped to stitch pieces of this together to form blankets of sorts. These crude attempts at supplying what most people would regard as basic necessities were touchingly rewarded. Tucked up for the night for the first time in months, the children cried with joy and excitement.

Every morning after prayers, all who could work did so – building bed frames, fetching coal or making straw sandals. Deacon Liu neglected his own business in order to help. His strictness with those who misbehaved was consistent with his love for them, since true love never lacks integrity or shrinks from taking a tough line when necessary.

At last there was a reply from Beijing. But it revealed the uncaring face of officialdom. No help would be forthcoming since, in the view of the authorities concerned, the famine had not come about 'through natural causes but through opium and banditry'.

Conditions worsened. Thousands died of starvation and disease. And all the time, more and more people kept arriving at the city. Driven by hunger, they left their villages and walked for miles, only to find that there was no land of plenty waiting for them. Exhausted and starving, many lay down and died in the streets. Seeing them, Alfred was appalled to think of all the food thrown away daily by people back home in England.

Some money began to come in from the mission and the Beijing Relief Fund. Jack decided to use it to buy coal, but at a fair price, hoping this would encourage others to do likewise and ease the plight of those dependent on its sale. In the temple, mothers ground corn and cereals to make puddings to sell at nominal prices along with the rice porridge.

Misery and fear often make fertile breeding grounds for scapegoating, usually of minorities or 'outsiders'. So, in famine-ridden Zunyi, rumour had it that the missionaries had evil or at least ulterior motives. According to one story, they planned to export the children to England or America; and to another, they were fattening them up for food!

Alfred was hurt and horrified – not just for himself but also for the Chinese Christians who had been selflessly and lovingly putting the children's needs before their own.

'What can we do?' he asked Jack Robinson.

'Pray,' was the wise, quiet response.

In the end, only a few mothers believed the rumours and left the temple; and Alfred was able to write home and say, 'We seem to have the goodwill of the people generally despite the anti-foreign movement.'

But there was no easing up on other fronts. Sickness, perhaps brought by newcomers to the refuge, swept through the place, affecting the children. Many became ill with fever and diarrhoea. Of these, eight died.

Then a boy contracted smallpox. He was quickly segregated. But fear of the dread disease now gripped everyone.

Something else they feared, and with good reason, was drought. The people flocked to their gilded wing-roofed temples to perform elaborate rituals, in an attempt to soften the hearts of their deities and cause them to send rain.

Nothing happened. Even more destitute people filled the streets; of these, as many as possible were squeezed into the refuge. There were now a hundred homeless people to feed and care for.

'Our money will last for another month,' Alfred wrote home. 'Some of the officials have promised support but have never paid. To date we have had fifteen deaths in the refuge; all but two were small children.'

LIFE AND DEATH

At last, in July, the rains fell, turning the main street into a river for a time, cleansing the city and bringing new life and hope to the people. Welcome as they were, these late rains could not undo all the damage caused by the drought, so only half a harvest was expected. Meanwhile more children died in the refuge.

Jack Robinson, a music-lover like Alfred, had long been saving up for a gramophone, eagerly anticipating the joy of listening to the singing of Ernest Lough or the music of oratorios with church choirs and organs. But while people starved such luxuries could not possibly be justified. The money went into buying wheat to make more puddings to feed the hungry and no further reference was made to what it might have been spent on.

One day Alfred brought a sad and ill-nourished six-year-old boy into the refuge. His mother and older brother had died, and he had no knowledge of his father's existence or whereabouts. Mr Liu offered to pay for a month's board for him, and Alfred put him in a bath and applied carbolic soap to his ingrained dirt.

But before long the application of love achieved something even more important than cleanliness. Slowly it dawned on the child that the missionary loved him. At first he kept gazing at Alfred, not quite daring to believe that such a wonderful thing could be true.

Then he became sick with fever and stomach trouble, and Alfred sat beside him and, along with others, helped to care for him. Gradually the boy recovered physically, but the biggest change was emotional. The dour, suspicious six-year-old became a happy, trusting child, who smiled and laughed and sang as he busied himself helpfully around the place. He was devoted to the missionary, and would sit and listen to his prayers, chipping in to remind him of who or what he had forgotten to mention.

The sight of this boy brought a crumb of comfort to Alfred as he grieved for the children they *hadn't* been able to help – those who had died in the refuge. If not for everyone, for this one child at least they had changed the world.

By the end of the year, rice was scarce again and therefore costly. Alfred found it a tragic irony to have to use his brand new typewriter, a gift from friends in Manchester, for typing out a newsletter which virtually echoed his account of the previous year's traumas.

The missionaries and Mr Liu went about the city and visited the new refugee shelters opened by the city authorities. What they found there imprinted itself indelibly on their memories. A man begging for the money he needed to bury his wife. Dozens of people, half-dead from cold and hunger, crammed into a shelter and huddled around one tiny fire. The slight body of a mere boy left at the door of a refuge, where he had collapsed and died. Two small children, little more than skeletons themselves, sitting on a dead body. Two corpses, stripped and left naked by callous or desperate robbers, being eaten by rats.

With the wheat harvest still five months away, it was clear that the Christians would have to restart the feeding programme. They transferred the refuge from the temple to a large house and started taking in the homeless and destitute. Alfred was put in charge of the boys. From the money donated by the local army general and by people in England, rice was purchased for feeding the people in the refuge and for free distribution to homes in the village. Out of a hundred homes to which Mr Liu took rice, eighty had no other food whatsoever.

In the midst of all the misery, Adeline Robinson gave birth to a third son. 'In the eyes of the Chinese she is indeed fortunate to have three sons,' wrote Alfred, 'but she was wanting a daughter!'

Then came snow and savage cold, claiming yet more lives. The boys' refuge was full but Alfred found it impossible to turn away desperate children. He gave up his three hours' language study and trusted that talking informally with the children would serve the purpose instead.

Zunyi received a visit from the chairman of Guizhou's famine relief committee. In appalled anger, he stood outside a shelter and watched scavenging dogs feeding on human corpses left lying in the street. A local authority that could allow such things to happen was not to be trusted with administering relief. He asked Jack Robinson and a Catholic priest to handle it instead, with Alfred as the inspector responsible for overseeing food distribution and burial of the dead.

The missionaries were quite busy enough without these added duties. But they took them on and fulfilled them as best they could with insufficient resources. They were given straw mats as bed coverings for the children, but these were small defence against the freezing night air. Jack caught flu and many of the children suffered from pains and headaches. With little or no medicine available, treatment was out of the question for most of them.

Alfred felt close to breaking point. Then he became desperately ill, burning up with fever and delirious at times, convinced that he would die. Jack sent a telegram to the nearest doctor. He diagnosed typhus. Being a journey of eight days away he didn't offer to come in person for the crisis would be over, one way or another, before his arrival.

Jack and Adeline bathed Alfred daily to try to reduce his temperature. For five days he was unconscious and, during that time, his hair fell out. But his colleagues and the Chinese Christians prayed, believing that he would pull through.

On the fifth day, they heard him shout out, 'Lord, save me!' When they came into his room, they found him sleeping peacefully.

In a letter to Heinrich and Marie Bosshardt, Jack wrote, 'It was touching to see the solicitude of some of the Chinese Christians for Alfred's recovery. There is a scourge of typhus in this province and hundreds of deaths among all classes. In his delirium Alfred frequently prayed and sang hymns, while his first request on recovery was for his Bible; your letters I have kept for him until he is a little stronger.'

Eight days later Alfred began to take an interest in what was going on and got out of bed for a short time. On Easter Day he managed a brief outing to the garden, where he feasted his senses on the delicate beauty of trees in blossom and the vivid splendour of the roses which he had planted the previous year.

Two food parcels arrived, sent by Union Hall, Manchester. Intended as Christmas gifts, their arrival just then proved very timely. Swiss cheese, tongue, dried fruit, biscuits, sweets and chocolate: just what was needed to tempt the invalid's slowly returning appetite. Alfred wanted to share everything, but his colleagues were adamant that this food was God's gift to aid his recovery.

Even so, the process of returning to full health and strength was slow – and the restrictions which at that time were thought necessary were an added frustration. Presumed to be highly contagious until his skin had peeled, he was isolated for almost three months, confined to his room and not even allowed to write letters home.

Eventually, his hair grew back and he even, round about this time, began to sport a neat moustache – a fashion to which he was to remain faithful for the rest of his life.

By the time he was out of quarantine and better, the famine conditions were not so acute in Guizhou. Food was more readily available, though the cost of living soared.

As soon as he was in the clear Alfred wrote home in high spirits and from an overflowing heart:

'O, magnify the Lord with me and let us exalt his name together. You will have heard of the way the Lord has had compassion on me. It has been a great trial not to be able to write to you. I am taking the first opportunity, but if I write all that is in my heart this will not be a letter but a book.'

He also wrote to the mission headquarters in Shanghai expressing deep appreciation of Jack and Adeline's care of him. The letter he received in response to this urged him to spend plenty of time in the open air and avoid getting overtired. It went on, 'Thank you for your appreciative words with reference to the Robinsons' care of you. The Lord will reward all such labours, for inasmuch as they have done it unto you, they have done it unto him.'

A SWISS ROSE

In a country renowned for its watchmaking, the Piaget works at La Côte-aux-Fées in the Jura mountains of Switzerland had a world-wide reputation for excellence. It was in this setting that Mama Piaget gave birth to seventeen children, of whom fourteen – seven of each sex – survived into adulthood. Rose, the sixth girl, was born in 1894.

In terms of family and church background Rose and Alfred had much in common. Her family were committed Christians who joined other like-minded individuals and families at the lively, outgoing Free Church for Sunday services and other meetings. It was a church that supported missions, and at a missionary meeting there one evening Rose sensed that God was calling her to China.

Louisa Köhler, back in her homeland for the one furlough she was to take in her fifty years as a missionary, was the speaker. As she talked of her work with CIM in Guizhou, Rose's heart was won and her will engaged. In the next years she steadily set her course for China – pursuing her profession as a nurse and midwife, and then going for Bible training to St Chrischona.

In 1920, at the age of twenty-six, she arrived in Shanghai and, after language study in Yangzhou, Jiangsu province, was assigned to work in the south-west. Miss Köhler herself escorted the young woman from Shanghai to Guizhou – a four-month journey fraught with danger and difficulty, through poor communications, bad travelling conditions and the ever-present threat of bandits. Significantly, right from the start, Rose knew what it was like to have to trust God in situations of fear and uncertainty.

'It is with profound thanksgiving,' she wrote, 'that I can look back and review the road the Lord has led me. He has done miracles for me. He has sent angels before me and protected me. He is looking after me and preparing me for his service.' Her words, typically, were straight from the heart, reflecting her simple but profound faith.

In Guiyang, capital of Guizhou, she was to continue learning Chinese – a task which she did not find easy. But after two years she was able to take her first Sunday School lesson in the language: the story of God calling the child Samuel to deliver a difficult message from him. With teaching and book-selling, working in the hospital and visiting the women's prison, her days were fully occupied.

Her next appointment, in 1925, was to Zhenyuan, further east, not far from the borders of Hunan province. Here life was more hazardous. Armed robbers constantly terrorised the people with their looting, kidnapping and gun battles.

On top of that, famine swept through the district, causing widespread starvation, sickness and death. While Alfred battled with typhus, Rose cared for forty orphans.

At the same time, anti-foreign feeling was running high, forcing some missionaries to leave the country. Rose managed to complete her first seven years before taking home leave, going back to her large, loving family and peaceful homeland for a much-needed change and rest.

She returned this time to Chongqing and prepared to set off for Guizhou with two of her colleagues. Meanwhile Alfred had received a message asking him to go to Chongqing to escort three women missionaries back to Guizhou.

He was far from keen on the idea, having just returned to Guizhou after taking two women, one seriously ill, from there to Chongqing. The trip had included a hair-raising journey by boat on a river full of rapids and two encounters with bandits in which most of their luggage had been stolen and Alfred had been kidnapped.

In the end he'd been released and they'd all reached Chongqing safely. But the last thing Alfred wanted to do was to run another three women into danger. Then he discovered the names of the women concerned – and changed his tune. *Certainly* he would escort them back to their mission stations!

Years earlier Peter Olesen had told Alfred that a lovely Swiss girl called Rose Piaget would be just the right wife for him. At the time, not having seen the lady in question, Alfred had responded coolly. But his senior missionary was nothing if not persistent. When the Robinsons had come to take over the station, he had suggested that Alfred should accompany him to Guiyang and so give the new missionaries time to settle in on their own. Though not fooled for one moment by this ploy, Alfred had felt obliged to go along with it.

And so he had gone to Guiyang and met Rose. She was indeed lovely – a petite and elegant brunette with a sweet smile and gentle manner, who spoke English with a delightful French accent. Clearly they had much in common and he had been strongly attracted to her. But was she God's choice for him? For Alfred this, as always, had been the crucial question.

Returning to his work at Zunyi, he had often thought and prayed about Rose. But the famine, his illness, and finally Rose's furlough had effectively kept them apart. Now, unexpectedly, their paths were to cross again.

The party set off – three women in sedan chairs, Alfred on foot, and twenty porters carrying the luggage. The journey, though less dramatic than the previous one, was not without incident. One porter absconded with some of Rose's things. The baskets in which these had been carried were later recovered from a wood but most of their contents had been removed.

Alfred, so the story ran later, had had his eye on the *lady* rather than on the luggage. At the time, however, he said nothing to Rose about his feelings, although she was very much on his mind.

Was it fair to marry, he wondered. Life in China was precarious, and might well prove short, and he had already turned thirty. Was he worthy of someone as special as Rose? But in the end he had to know the answer, one way or another, to the vital question: would she marry him?

He proposed by letter. Rose was not an impulsive girl, but a mature woman who wanted to be sure that any decision she took was the right one, whatever her own feelings in the matter. She thought and prayed over the letter for two weeks, as well as consulting her senior missionary.

It had been a long fortnight's wait for Alfred. But as soon as Rose's letter of acceptance arrived he set off eagerly to visit her. Being a dutiful and loving daughter, she naturally wanted parental approval and asked Alfred to write to her 'family council' – as she laughingly designated the Piagets back home. He duly wrote asking permission to marry Rose, and she translated the letter into French and sent it off to La Côte-aux-Fées.

Alfred also wrote to his parents, but in ecstatic vein and with little doubt of their consent. 'I have asked Miss Rose Piaget to be my wife ... I wish I had a nice photograph of her to send to you. I am sure you would fall in love with her too.'

The response from both sets of parents was positive. Plans were made for Alfred to take a short home leave and then return for the marriage.

In April 1930, he sailed down the Yangzi on the SS *Ping Wo*. It was on this journey that the ship's first officer emerged from his cabin to find the missionary utterly transfixed by the beautiful music issuing from there. He invited Alfred in to take a look at the source of the sounds which had so captivated him, and was astonished to learn that his guest had never even seen a radio up until that moment.

Alfred had made up his mind to learn French, so as to be able to get closer to Rose and communicate with her family. On the long boat trip to England, he spent many hours on the language. His eventual fluency was to have very unexpected and remarkable consequences.

Meantime, as well as studying, he had the opportunity to rest and enjoy the food and the company, the sea and the sun. But he longed for Rose to be there beside him, marvelling too at the luminous flame colours of the sunset, or watching the flying fish skimming the waves with the sun shimmering on their scales.

Back in Manchester at last, Alfred was reunited with his family in the modern semi in Chorlton-cum-Hardy to which his parents and Ida had moved soon after his departure for China. Frieda's loss was keenly felt, but there were two new members to meet − a brother-in-law and a nephew. Arthur Brunnschweiler, a Swiss businessman, had married Lily in 1924 and they lived nearby with their first child, David.

The whole family gathered to celebrate Heinrich's seventieth birthday. It was a happy time, but Alfred was aware that the years had brought a shift in focus. China had become his home: he was a visitor everywhere else.

His next port of call was La Côte-aux-Fées. Rose's father, a skilled craftsman, was now very weak and old; blind, too, as a result of diabetes. He and his wife and their large family sat around the dining-room table with a somewhat apprehensive Alfred. But he was quickly reassured and made to feel at home. In fact, the Piagets and their vibrant church fellowship, lovely village and beautiful country were to be very special and important in his life.

TOGETHER

Alfred and Rose were married in June 1931, in a chapel in Guiyang. In the unavoidable absence of family members on this very special occasion in their lives – something they accepted as part of the cost of their calling – there were plenty of English and Chinese friends and well-wishers.

They were a good-looking couple – Alfred of medium height and build, with blue-grey eyes and brown hair and moustache, and Rose a whole head shorter, petite and chic, with dark hair and brown eyes.

The bride's shoes were of embroidered white satin but the rest of her outfit reflected more of the European tradition: a loose fitting skirt and top, with a long veil, all white – a colour worn only at funerals in China. The groom was dressed in Chinese style: long white gown, black jacket and small black cap.

The service too paid tribute to both cultures, being partly in English and partly in Chinese, with a Welsh minister performing the ceremony assisted by a Chinese elder. Other countries were also represented, as Alfred's best man was a New Zealander and Rose's two bridesmaids were Chinese and Swedish American respectively, her matron of honour being Louisa Köhler from Switzerland.

Afterwards seventy friends gathered for a fourteen-course Chinese feast. The honeymoon was in Qingzhen, eighteen miles away. The journey there was part of the celebration, as they travelled in ceremonial sedan chairs borne swiftly along by alternating teams of porters. The Christians greeted the arrival of the newly-weds by setting off fire-crackers. By midnight they were alone at last.

After the honeymoon came the joy of setting up their first home and working together in Zhenyuan. Very much in love, they grew more devoted as the years went by. They had a great deal in common. There was the Swiss connection, and their faith, commitment and calling. They also shared a love of music and enjoyed singing together.

In other ways they differed and complemented one another. As was traditional at that time, perhaps particularly in Christian circles, Alfred saw himself as the leader and protector, and Rose seemed happy to follow and support. Her call to the mission arose out of loving obedience and a caring nature rather than the lure of danger and adventure that had conquered Alfred's childhood imagination. But for all that and despite her slight physique and shy, gentle manner, she had, as time would show, tremendous reserves of courage and strength.

The couple kept in close touch with their families and friends. Letters, written and received, became a regular and vital part of their lives; a way in which links were strengthened as the correspondents shared their news, their hopes and dreams, joys and sorrows.

From Switzerland came news of Mama and Papa Piaget's golden wedding celebrations. Even with Rose abroad and a grandchild in hospital, there were sixty-one family members to celebrate the occasion, including eighteen grandsons and eighteen granddaughters. Papa was carried in a chair to the chapel and said a few words to his family. A few weeks later, he died peacefully.

In Zhenyuan, the newly-weds pursued their busy lives, visiting and getting to know the people, teaching and preaching the Christian message. Among the more common social or medical problems they encountered was opium smoking.

One addict known to Rose and Alfred became a Christian, but the craving did not disappear. He resisted it for a time. But the withdrawal symptoms persisted and became unbearable. On the fourth day, ready to admit defeat, he primed and lit his opium lamp and lay down for a smoke.

It was then that he became aware of a painful crick in his neck. This, he was convinced, was God's way of telling him not to smoke opium. He put the lamp away. Three more agonising days followed, then the craving weakened and almost went away, but not quite. In the weeks that followed, it returned from time to time, with decreasing severity. Finally he was free, and threw in his lot with the local church, to serve as a powerful example to others.

Lawlessness was another common problem for missionaries and Chinese alike. By now Alfred had had four encounters with bandits. Many other missionaries had similar experiences. The famous trio of Mildred Cable, Francesca and Evangeline French were arrested and held for months, only to continue their work the moment they were released.

Missionary colleagues Grace Emblen and Elizabeth Stair came to reopen the mission at Sinan. The Bosshardts travelled the twenty-five-day journey with them, then helped them to settle in. Alfred wrote with admiration of their faith and pluck: 'They were typical of women missionaries who pioneered the gospel in places where men would have feared.' Little did he realise what lay ahead for him and one of them.

Alfred and Rose ran some special meetings and saw people being affected by what they heard. Some became aware of their wrongdoing and were anxious to receive forgiveness. The colporteur's young son tearfully confessed to his father that he had been stealing from him for years, as well as swearing and lying at school. Then the two of them knelt and prayed together. An hour's beating wouldn't have elicited such a confession from his son, the father assured Rose and Alfred. 'Only the Holy Spirit,' he added, 'could have led my boy to humble himself like that.'

There were others who responded similarly. But in general the work among the Chinese seemed relatively discouraging. Thousands of tribespeople were turning to God but only a few hundred Chinese in towns and cities. The missionary in charge of Guizhou province decided to call for more prayer for the Chinese.

Alfred and Rose joined other missionaries for this purpose at Anshun, south-west of Zhenyuan. After much prayer, some fasting, and deep heart-searching, the delegates drew up and signed a letter which was to be sent to the churches. It acknowledged that they, the Western missionaries, had failed in some areas. They had been remiss about handing over responsibility and positions of authority to the local Christians, and about accepting their true role as servants; they had not listened to God as they should have done.

The Bosshardts had come to the conference feeling very sad. Both of them loved and wanted children, and had been thrilled when Rose had become pregnant. But then she had had a miscarriage. In the midst of their grief and disappointment, God spoke to them during their times of quiet prayer. To Alfred, the message was, 'We are more than conquerors through him that loved us.' To Rose: 'All power is given unto me in heaven and in earth … and lo, I am with you always, even unto the end of the world.'

Afterwards, in response to rumours of trouble, the couple decided to return home via Jiuzhou, where they would be able to stay with fellow-missionaries, Arnolis and Rhoda Hayman.

Sunday with the Haymans and Grace Emblen proved to be a happy time. Despite their own disappointment, Alfred and Rose were able to enjoy the company of two of the Haymans' children, Frances and Ben, the four older ones – Theo, Joy, David and Andrew – being at school in Chefoo at the time. Alfred preached morning and evening to large numbers of people and was encouraged by the responsiveness of his hearers.

The next day was October 1st, 1934 – exactly twelve years since Alfred had first left for China. Arnolis Hayman escorted his guests and those accompanying them out of the city. With the Bosshardts were six Chinese people: their cook, Su En-lin – an orphan rescued as a boy from the streets some years earlier by Alfred; the Haymans' cook, a young woman named Li Gung-jing, who had been unwell; and the four porters who had been hired to carry the luggage and Rose's sedan chair.

Two roads lay ahead of them. After discussion, they took the one they thought would be the safer. But when they had nearly arrived at their destination for the night, a raiding party descended on them and proceeded to overpower them and seize their possessions – pens, watches, rings, bedding, money, clothes, books.

While Rose's mountain chair was being ransacked, she attempted to retrieve the Bibles but thought better of it when she saw one of the men purposefully loading his revolver.

'Don't shoot,' she told him. 'Take anything you want.'

Communication was not easy, as the raiders spoke the Jiangxi dialect. Undeterred by this, Alfred informed his captors in his south-western Mandarin that they would have to answer to God for the evil they were doing unless they repented. Their response was to bind one of his arms and march him downhill towards the village. Rose, he was relieved to notice, was unharmed and not far behind him.

The village was full of people. The bandits, if that's what they were, included some women as well as men. They were all wearing long, peaked caps with the insignia of a five-pointed star. Their jackets and trousers were similar in style but of many different colours – blue, grey, purple, green or yellow.

Alfred saw that the walls of the houses were covered in slogans. Huge Chinese characters proclaimed: 'Down with landlords and capitalists!' 'Religion is the opiate of the people!' 'The Soviet government is the only hope of China!' 'Take Chiang Kai-shek alive!'

Now he knew who their captors really were. Not bandits but Communists!

For years the Chinese Communists had been extremely active, not least in Hunan under the vigorous leadership of a peasant's son turned political activist, Mao Zedong. For a time the Party had even joined forces with the Government, also known as Nationalists or the Kuomintang, in order to rid the country of foreign domination and establish law and order. But soon after their joint armies, under Chiang Kai-shek, had completed the Northern Expedition against warlords, the uneasy alliance had collapsed and hostilities had been resumed.

Like most others, Alfred had not been fully aware of these events, let alone their significance. He had heard reports of sporadic fighting between the Nationalist troops and the Communist forces, or Red Army, but had assumed that the Government had the upper hand.

It had certainly looked that way earlier in the year, when Chiang's troops had blockaded the Red Army soldiers in Jiangxi. But then, putting their secret plan into action, the Communists had begun to evacuate their Jiangxi base with a view to setting up a new soviet elsewhere.

It was some time before the Nationalists, let alone the outside world, realised what was happening. By then the epic journey, to be known later as the Long March, was well under way. For the moment, Otto Braun, the German adviser from Russia, was in charge of tactics and strategy. But Mao Zedong was in the wings, biding his time – certain that he would soon be proved right about taking the Communist revolution not to the cities but to the countryside, where the poor, downtrodden, landless peasants comprising eighty per cent of the population were ripe for revolution; and right about employing guerilla tactics against the enemy.

Meanwhile, Alfred and Rose had unwittingly got caught up in the early stages of the Long March and were now prisoners of the Sixth Army under the command of General Xiao Ke.

Alfred Bosshardt in 1920 aged 23, when he took his first big step of faith, left work at a time when jobs were scarce, and went into missionary training with the China Inland Mission.

Rose Bosshardt as a young woman.

Alfred (right) during his first posting, and a colleague from New Zealand, Harry Taylor, in Zunyi, northern Guizhou 1927-31.

A group of Christians in Zunyi 1924-27. Alfred is in the back row, fourth from the left. Peter Olesen is in the middle of the front row and Deacon Liu is in the middle row, second from the left.

Alfred and Rose Bosshardt (née Piaget) on their wedding day. Alfred is wearing a very smart version of his usual black Chinese jacket and cap, with long loose white trousers. Rose is in a white two-piece with white satin shoes. The veil was a gift from her sisters back home in Switzerland.

CHINA AND THE WEST:
THE LONG MARCH AND
ONWARDS – 1934-1940

A LONG DAY

The captives were taken to a large stable. There, in the best traditions of the Red Army, most of their possessions were returned to them. Alfred spoke to one of the officials about God but he countered with, 'Who is your God to let you fall into our hands?'

'Perhaps,' Alfred replied, 'he has sent me to bear witness for him so that you may know he is the living God.'

Later he was taken to a house and interrogated by a Sixth Army judge named Wu – a man with whose volatile temper he was to become well acquainted.

'What are you doing in China?' Judge Wu asked Alfred.

'We came to China to preach and teach about God.'

This produced an incredulous laugh, and the response, 'We know about you missionaries! You're capitalist spies sent out by your imperial government to spy out China. That's a capital offence and we should execute you. But we won't execute you. We'll treat you mildly and only fine you 100,000 dollars each.'

'200,000 dollars – impossible!' Alfred gasped.

Ignoring this, the judge ordered him to write letters conveying this demand to the Swiss consul, the mission and the church at Zhenyuan. Alfred knew that mission policy was against paying ransoms, not least because doing so signalled to every opportunist that kidnapping missionaries would be a good way of earning easy money. Nevertheless, he penned the letters, knowing that they would convey information and prompt prayer.

For some time he had been aware of a woman – the judge's wife, he assumed – sitting on a bed and watching the proceedings. Ignoring her tough appearance, he spoke to her and found her to be a pleasant, well-educated person. He decided to put in a plea for Rose. Quietly he told her of his fear that his wife would not be able to stand the travelling, and that a soldier's life would be too much for her.

The woman's expression hardened as she responded, 'She'll have to rough it as I do.' They all roughed it that night – soldiers and prisoners, crammed together at close quarters. Rose shared a narrow plank bed with the Haymans' cook Li Gung-jing, while Alfred made himself as comfortable as possible in an upright chair.

Very early the next day, after a breakfast of rice and cabbage, the party was on the move to Jiuzhou. Alfred longed to warn the Haymans of the Red Army's approach, but was powerless to do so.

The city was only defended by the local militia – no match for the well-armed Red Army soldiers who soon swarmed over the walls to take possession of the place. The 'rich' city inhabitants were captured and their property and goods redistributed to the 'poor', after the victorious troops had taken their spoils. Mission premises, both Protestant and Catholic, were ransacked. The priests were safe, having managed to get away from their compound just in time. But Grace Emblen and the Haymans were caught and held as prisoners while the soldiers went through their rooms and offices, appropriating their personal possessions and household and office equipment.

Afterwards the new prisoners were moved in with the Bosshardts. Judge Wu, General Xiao Ke and two other officers came in and ordered Arnolis Hayman and Grace Emblen to write to their consuls, the mission and their local government chairman stating the terms of their release: a fine of 100,000 dollars each, including the children, amounting to a total of 500,000.

The officials left and Rose said eagerly, 'I've a message from God,' and read out the Bible verse: 'Our soul is escaped as a bird out of the snare of the fowlers: the snare is broken and we are escaped. Our help is in the name of the Lord, who made heaven and earth.' The next day, when the four porters were allowed to go, it seemed that the promise was being fulfilled.

Alfred and Arnolis Hayman approached Judge Wu to ask that the women and children should also be set free. His response, though not all they were hoping for, was quite a concession. He was prepared to release Rose and Rhoda with little Frances and baby Ben. But Grace Emblen was to remain a prisoner, along with the two cooks Li Gung-jing and Su En-lin, Alfred and Arnolis. All three 'foreigners' were needed to 'represent' their countries of origin — Canada, Switzerland and New Zealand. The fine, however, would still be for all seven of them, and hence remain at a total of 700,000 dollars.*

Behind the bed-curtains, Alfred and Rose snatched a moment of privacy to say their goodbyes. Both had a deep sense of inner peace but rather different expectations. Alfred felt it wouldn't be very long before they were reunited; Rose feared she might never see her husband again.

It was several days before Rhoda and the children and Rose were able to leave Jiuzhou. But then friends with cars were able to give them lifts which speeded them on their way. Rhoda and the children arrived safely in Shanghai and Rose in Guangzhou, where she stayed for a time at a school for blind children. From there, on October 31st, she wrote to Alfred's parents.

'I have heard nothing about our dear ones in captivity. It is today exactly a month that we met with this greatest trial of our faith. It is the greatest, dear parents. May our dear and faithful Lord sustain you as he does me...

'At the school they have been celebrating American Thanksgiving Day. It was all so very interesting and one was amazed at the beautiful singing. In the evening we went to a concert in another part of the city.

---

*About £45,000.

I have not been to many concerts in my life. I thought how much dear Alfred would have enjoyed the piano and the flute. The lady singer imitated the lark and was in perfect harmony with the flute. My tears rolled down my cheeks, I could not restrain them for thinking of my dear husband, he loves music so...

'Dr Hayes has discovered that my throat is probably the cause of my deafness. Tonsils are in a bad state. I praise the Lord for bringing me here and having the opportunity for treatment.

'I am confused at the great loving-kindness of the Lord. Surely he cares for dear Alfred and the others, and will not permit that they suffer above their strength. Be not anxious but pray. It is only prayer that shall help our dear captives through and bring them out if it is God's will and in his own time.'

It was to be a long time before the captives had any news of their loved ones. Meanwhile they were numb with shock and anguish, totally out of sorts with the jubilation all around them. The Sixth Army celebrated its easy capture of Jiuzhou with a feast of fresh pork, seaweed and eggs, and then moved on, with its prisoners and plunder. Some of the comrades were twirling bright paper umbrellas or wearing newly acquired woolly hats or shoes. One man had made a cape for himself out of a Catholic altar-cloth.

Miserably, Alfred struggled and slipped along paths made treacherous by recent rain. Arnolis was somewhere up ahead, but Grace was nearby and Alfred helped her for as long as he was allowed to. Then he asked Su En-lin to stay behind with her. A mountain chair was eventually found for her, but the porters kept complaining that she was too heavy to carry and making her get out and walk.

Even Alfred and Arnolis who were used to walking quite long distances, found it impossible to match the pace of the Red Army soldiers. Mostly very young, they kept up a tremendous jogging speed, thinking nothing of doing forty miles in a day. Fortunately, they only covered fifteen miles on that first day.

They stopped at a village. But instead of being allowed to rest, the missionaries had their first experience of being treated as exhibits. On arrival, the propaganda squad set about plastering the walls of houses with Communist slogans. Then they made the missionaries sit on chairs in the village street, wearing placards. Arnolis was designated 'Britisher' and Alfred 'Swiss'. When Grace arrived, she too was exhibited but without a placard. Perhaps the propagation squad didn't know the Chinese characters for 'Canada' or was unsure of that country's attitude towards Communism, and hence of the correct Party line towards its citizens.

As local people gathered round, and the soldiers kept arriving, the squad played music and spoke to them about the great Communist party. To the troops, they called out, 'Comrades, you have suffered much hardship during recent days, so we have a gramophone for your entertainment. And over here are some imperialist spies, sent by their governments to spy out and slice up China. They used the preaching of the Christian religion as a cloak for their activities. But we have won a great victory over these foreigners and now their religious society is going to have to pay a large sum of money for them...'

The missionaries found themselves surrounded by people staring, laughing and shouting verbal abuse at them. 'Foreign devil', 'hook nose', 'imperialist spy' were among the more popular taunts. Some tried to grab the prisoners' noses or bully them physically, but the officials restrained them.

Alfred reminded himself that he and his colleagues were in good company. Jesus Christ was scorned and falsely accused. He, too, must have longed to see one kind, gentle face among all the hard, hostile ones.

Wearily lifting his head, Alfred scanned the surrounding faces. In one or two he read a hint of sympathy or distress. But most of the spectators appeared to be unmoved by their plight, if not actually enjoying or contributing to it. 'The Lord loves you and died for you': Alfred repeated the words silently while focusing on the face of one of his tormentors. He did this again and again. Each time, the same thing happened. His negative emotions were replaced by love. What was more, as he put it, 'I don't remember anyone repeating an insult when I was looking at them like that.'

At last the ordeal was over and the missionaries were allowed to lie down and sleep on mounds of grain, with the ever-present armed guard nearby. A makeshift lamp, using lard and strips of cloth, was kept going all night.

DECISION BY NIGHT

Alfred and Arnolis slept badly after their first day with the Red Army. Early the next morning they were woken by their guards and soon the long procession was on its way. Looking around, Arnolis recognised some of his possessions being carried or put to use by their captors. It was painful to see that Ben's cot quilt was now a saddle-rug for a woman Communist leader; and galling also to know that his duplicator would help to produce the Party's publicity material.

That night the missionaries were billeted in a Buddhist temple. They were put in the room behind the idols and given a small charcoal fire against the cold. Before Alfred could go to sleep, a messenger arrived to say that General Xiao Ke would like to see him.

It had been a long day. With no inkling of how significant the coming encounter would be, Alfred walked wearily along, wondering what the general wanted of him.

At a personal level, he had already warmed to this fit, fine-looking young man, sensing some of the qualities which had earned him the respect and admiration of his soldiers. In the months ahead his intelligence, courage and determination, high ideals and leadership ability, were to become increasingly evident.

For the moment, Alfred having arrived at the General's quarters, the two men faced one another: captive and captor, differing in status, background and outlook, but both passionately sincere in their beliefs and equally committed to their goals.

Xiao Ke greeted his prisoner courteously, then showed him a large map — evidently a recent acquisition — of Guizhou province. It was detailed and accurate but, as the General pointed out, in a foreign language. Would Alfred be willing to translate the words into Chinese, he asked.

It was an unexpected request. Alfred stared thoughtfully down at the map, noting that it was in French and had therefore probably been taken as part of the plunder from a Catholic mission station. As he spoke both French and Chinese, he was in a unique position to do as Xiao Ke asked. But the question was — should he? Would his conscience allow him to? He had to make a quick decision by night and very much in the dark as to the possible military and personal repercussions, either way.

After a brief moment of hesitation, he told the General he would help him. Xiao Ke thanked him, but Alfred had no inkling of the depth of the General's gratitude and relief.

Up until then his troops had had to travel more or less 'blind', guided only by crude, inadequate maps found in school textbooks. The local people had been unable to help in the matter. Apart from being in the main illiterate, and perhaps high on opium as well, they tended to be insular, unaware of what was going on outside their own backyards. With Alfred's help, Xiao Ke would now be able to locate exactly where they were and to plan the Red Army's route strategically, avoiding main roads and Nationalist strongholds.

But there was more to it than that. That night's encounter and decision were to mark the beginning of a change of attitude in the General — one which was to deepen and become profound as Xiao Ke subsequently observed the character and conduct of both Alfred and Arnolis. The ensuing repercussions would be a long time coming but dramatic.

For almost the whole night, by lamplight, Alfred worked on the map, the General sitting opposite him, listening intently and asking questions.

Finally, his task conscientiously completed, he was able to rejoin

Arnolis and Grace. Together they drew strength from God through praying, singing hymns and reading from their Chinese Bible.

On their first Sunday in captivity the sound of firing brought them to a halt, then had them beating a hasty retreat across the mountains. When they were allowed to stop, the hard, steep hillsides made rest difficult and sleep impossible.

The two men became increasingly concerned about Grace. Once she lost her footing and fell several feet before being caught and held by a clump of sturdy mountain shrubs. On another day she fainted with exhaustion.

But she kept reading the Bible verses in her *Daily Light*, ready to hear God speaking to her, giving her strength and courage. One day she read out to her colleagues words that echoed her feelings: 'None of these things move me, neither count I my life dear unto myself, so that I might finish my course with joy.' But while her spiritual stamina increased, her physical condition continued to deteriorate.

'Set her free,' Alfred and Arnolis prayed with compassionate urgency. They also spoke on her behalf to Judge Wu and his wife, travelling near them in the centre of the column. But their response was abruptly dismissive.

A few nights later Alfred and Arnolis were resting, expecting Grace and her party to arrive at any time. After about two hours all they had seen was her empty chair. Very concerned, but forced to move on, the two men could only pray for her.

Much later they were to learn how their prayers had been answered. Grace was at the end of her strength and lagging behind badly, when an inner voice prompted her to 'stand still and see the salvation of the Lord which he will show you today'.

Su En-lin, who had faithfully stuck by the missionary ever since Alfred had put her in his care, added his advice. Having previously heard the soldiers say something to one another about abandoning the foreigner, he now urged Grace to slow down even further rather than do her best to catch up. She readily complied, at which the guards, instead of nagging or coming back for the stragglers, proceeded to turn a blind eye and press on. Before long, Grace and Su En-lin found themselves alone – free to make their way to Zhenyuan and safety.

Unaware of this, Alfred and Arnolis were overtaken at dawn by Grace's guards. 'She's been set free,' they said. But the missionaries could only be cautiously optimistic: the phrase 'set free' was sometimes a euphemistic allusion to someone's execution. It was to be a long time before they heard the full story.

In the meantime, they feared for the Haymans' cook Li Gung-jing, who was being bullied by the guards. Cursed, threatened with beatings and even death, she refused to deny her Christian faith. This went on for eleven days. Then, much to the relief of the missionaries, the Chinese woman was released – charged with the duty of delivering letters demanding radio parts and foreign medicine in exchange for the two men. These official letters, for whatever reason, never reached their destination, but the personal ones which she smuggled out did – and were avidly read by Rose and Rhoda.

To Rose, Alfred had written:

'There has been fighting and retreat and silent marching in the dark but as our days so has our strength been and so it shall be. We have not been troubled with vermin and the food is generally free from red pepper.

'I have not the time now to go into any details of our journeys, but we have passed through most magnificent country and I can revel in God's wonderful handiwork. Pray on and may all the dear friends do so and God will manifest his power to deliver out of the hand of the enemy. O, I am so glad you were spared this trial! For we who can walk it is more like a picnic.'

Brave words, indeed!

When darkness fell hurricane lamps and makeshift torches were lit and held aloft, creating a moving line of dancing flames and glowing spheres.

One night enemy troops were spotted in the valley below. So instant silence and the extinguishing of all lights was ordered. Plunged into darkness, the marchers then groped their way blindly forward, their hands resting on the shoulders of the people in front. Tantalisingly, government troops were so near and yet – there being no chance of escaping and gaining their protection – so far.

When the danger was past lanterns and torches were relit and a halt was called at a village. As there was not enough room to accommodate them in any of the houses, Alfred and Arnolis were put into a hastily constructed booth.

Sitting in this, they saw three terrified prisoners being marched along by their guards. Their hands were tied tightly behind their backs forcing their heads down. When some distance away, they were ordered to kneel. In this abject position they were beheaded by a very young soldier, who proceeded to clean his bloodstained sword on his victims' garments before strolling nonchalantly back with the guards.

The missionaries were sickened and saddened by the incident. That such a young man should be so hardened seemed to make it worse. Yet it was this same youth who had shown them kindness, on one occasion giving them a lump of salt for flavouring their food.

Alfred was to comment later that the members of the Red Army 'were not all cold-blooded, happy executioners, but some were fanatics who would take a man's life as casually as a chicken's – ruthlessly dedicated to what they saw as honourable designs'.

Many such incidents took place over the next months. Rather than having to witness them, the missionaries turned their faces away. For them, as for all Christians, every individual was immensely precious, because God so loved each one.

On the other hand the discipline and dedication, enthusiasm and commitment, of many of the Red Army soldiers made a deep impression on them. And later, Alfred would challenge Christians to be as zealous as the Communists while rejecting their willingness to use any means, however violent and cruel, to attain their ends.

One day, as they walked in heavy, drenching rain, Alfred's sandals, never a good fit, kept disintegrating from around his already sore and blistered feet. But on arrival at a village the guards lit a fire and everyone was able to rest and dry their clothes. Then an ox was killed and sliced up for food.

The next morning, just as the army was leaving, a guard handed Alfred and Arnolis a bowl filled with a good helping of the sliced raw beef. The missionaries marched all day carrying this generous gift, as they supposed it to be. In the evening they stewed and ate it, sharing some with their guards. It was a rare experience to sit by a glowing fire, savouring the aroma of cooking meat and, afterwards, to eat it and feel replete.

But soon the order to move on was given, and Alfred had to walk most of the next five miles with a bare right foot, one sandal having finally given up the ghost. The captain of the guard promised to attend to the matter. But in the morning, when it appeared that he had forgotten, Alfred wrapped his foot in cloth as best he could.

It was Judge Wu who noticed the missionary's makeshift footwear and ordered that something better should be found. Since the forced marches of recent weeks had allowed no time for anyone to make or repair sandals, there wasn't much on offer. In the end a soldier very reluctantly handed over his galoshes.

Alfred had every sympathy with him. Indeed, he felt guilty and unhappy about improving his own situation by making someone else's worse. And so, as he walked, he prayed for the unwilling donor and vowed never to take healthy feet or good shoes for granted again. 'In this life,' he was to write, 'comfort for one is often costly for another.'

Some time on this same day, the guard came and asked the missionaries to hand back the bowl of raw beef which he'd asked them to carry for him. It was a tricky moment, but fortunately the man was not too angry about the outcome of the misunderstanding.

Though frequently deprived of the food, sleep and rest that their bodies needed, Alfred and Arnolis received spiritual sustenance.

They prayed for their captors and fellow-prisoners, for their loved ones, colleagues and themselves; and they sang hymns and read the New Testament and *Daily Light*. They also made a practice of counting their blessings – recalling the day's events so as to pinpoint everything that had happened, however small, for which they could be grateful. By depending on God and drawing on his superhuman resources, they were saved from the corrosive effects of emotions such as hate, bitterness and self-pity.

For the moment Alfred and Arnolis were kept separate from the other prisoners, but it distressed them to see the way their fellow-captives were roped together and driven along by their guards. And there were other far worse sights to be endured along the way. The corpses of those whom the Red Army condemned and executed could often be seen rotting by the roadsides, the placards proclaiming their 'crimes' still attached to their decapitated bodies.

In the midst of all this, Alfred and Arnolis were often stretched to the limits of their endurance. Apart from the pace at which they often travelled, there were the 'roads' to contend with – the rough, uneven, often muddy footways criss-crossing the vast, flat plains, or the rugged, boulder-strewn, twisting mountain tracks. And sometimes they forded icy streams or crossed precarious bridges hastily improvised from doors and tables.

Stuck in the middle of the column, the missionaries were not directly involved in any fighting. But they heard the shooting, and smelt the smoke from the gunfire, when the soldiers at the rear or front of the column were attacking or defending themselves against government troops. And they sometimes saw the aftermath of battle dead or wounded soldiers and civilians; land and homes laid waste.

As the days went by and the missionaries listened to what was being said by their guards, they began to learn more about what they had been unwittingly caught up in. What was happening was not some local haphazard affair but part of a bigger enterprise. There were obviously several armies in touch with one another. If the Sixth Army was anything to go by, there must be tens of thousands of marchers. Soldiers, guards, civilian officials, doctors, porters, tailors, cooks, mechanics and other skilled and manual workers. All moving purposefully through the countryside. Feeding, clothing and financing themselves. Ready to attack and harass the enemy or beat a strategic retreat and live to fight another day. Recruiting for the Communist cause, spreading Party dogma and rule everywhere they went.

FOLLOWING THE FLAG

The Red Army entered Sichuan province. Resembling Guizhou with its high mountains, fast rivers and damp and misty climate, it was also rich in natural resources, and very heavily populated within the area known as the Sichuan basin where rice and other products grew in abundance.

Somewhere in the eastern part of the province Xiao Ke's Sixth Army achieved its objective of meeting up with General He Long's Second Army. The soldiers in this Second Army, Alfred noticed, were poorly dressed but very loyal to the cause, judging by all the red badges on their clothing and the Red Flags they were clutching.

The two armies celebrated their historic meeting by a day of feasting and fun, amid much band-playing and flag-waving. Surrounded by all this jollity and aware that they were now captives of two armies, Alfred and Arnolis felt increasingly dejected and insignificant. But there were compensations.

Being able to enjoy a full day's rest was sheer luxury, after twenty-seven days of being more or less constantly on the move, including two seventy-hour periods of non-stop marching. There were other luxuries too – honey bought locally, and the chance to wash their clothes and take a bath. This led to the unwelcome but hardly surprising discovery that they had lice.

Next day the march resumed – two armies combining as the Second Front Army under two commanders. Both men were good-looking and fine leaders but in different ways and with other marked contrasts between them. Xiao, aged twenty-six but totally bald through a childhood illness, came from an educated family in Hunan, and was rather a quiet, serious and scholarly person who wrote poetry. He also had the capacity for forethought and planning and the strength of character required for seeing things through. He Long, aged thirty-six, was from a poorer family in Sangzhi, had taught himself to read and write as an adult, and was a more extrovert, flamboyant character, with a penchant for the dramatic and the gift of oratory. Originally a Nationalist, he had joined the Communist cause soon after the Nanchang uprising in 1927, when he and Xiao Ke had first met.

Now, seven years later, the two Red Army generals were to work together well, respecting and complementing one another. In the course of the Long March they would marry sisters and each father a child – He Long a daughter and Xiao Ke a son.

For the moment, under their joint leadership, the Red Army headed for Youyang, where another rest was anticipated. But it was not to be. On arrival there the the soldiers learnt that government troops were in the vicinity, so it was a question of getting out of the city and out of range as quickly as possible.

By the time it was deemed safe to call a halt, Alfred and Arnolis were exhausted. To their relief they overheard the judge's wife suggesting that they be allowed to share a horse.

In the event it was a mule that was found for them. For the next three days they took it in turns to ride the animal, under the watchful eye of its very bad-tempered owner.

The home of a wealthy landowner was taken over for their next time of rest. True to form, the comrades appropriated whatever they wanted of the man's goods and called on the local peasants to help themselves to his stocks of grain. Watching this, Alfred asked a comrade, 'Where do you draw the line between peasant and landowner?'

The reply was, 'If someone tills his own soil, he's all right. If others work his land, he's an oppressor.' Thanks to this particular 'oppressor' the Red Army was able to feast on pork, duck and chicken.

Following the property redistribution came the 'trials' of those accused of oppressing the poor or committing any other offence against the Communist code of conduct. In some instances such accusations were a cover-up for the settling of personal grudges and vendettas.

Alfred and Arnolis watched with compassion as a young boy wept and shivered while making sandals − the punishment he had been given for alleged spying activities. He worked all day and well into the night. Every now and then he broke down and begged the officials to send for his mother who, he said, could prove his innocence.

But his 'judges' were unmoved, and he was executed the next day.

The missionaries fared much better than other prisoners. Their former guards had promised that they would be provided with horses when they were transferred to the Second Army. Disappointingly, this rarely happened. Also, for the first time, they had to submit to the humiliation and discomfort of being roped with the other prisoners when they travelled at night or in situations where escape attempts might be made.

But the cloth sandals with which they were issued were a definite improvement on the straw variety. And at the next farmhouse, while the other prisoners were put in a granary, they had a room in which there was a straw mattress on a wooden frame.

Best of all was an unexpected bonus. It came about because they were now required to walk directly behind the standard-bearer. On special occasions he would hold aloft the Communist flag − a bright red rectangle inset with a black star surrounding a hammer and sickle.

At all other times he would carry the flag furled and, the missionaries were quick to note, wrapped for protection in an oil painting of the Nativity, looted from some chapel or other en route.

'And so,' Alfred recalled later, 'we followed the Christmas star, like the wise men uncertain where it would finally lead us!'

Rain made the dirt roads treacherous, but the column kept going – men and women on foot or on horseback, with all their baggage and pack animals. Thousands of slipping feet or hooves sent mud flying in all directions. In this shared predicament 'our captors' – in Alfred's words – 'were quite considerate, and even went out of their way to help us.'

But though capable of instinctive kindness or fellow-feeling, they were hazy about the concept of love. The Chinese character for this word was seen inscribed on a roadside rock one day.

'What does that mean?' the guards asked. Alfred and Arnolis were amazed, for the questioners could read Chinese fluently. Then it dawned on them that 'love' was not a concept of any importance to the Communists and hence rarely appeared in their Party literature. By contrast, it was one of the first characters that missionaries taught in their classes for illiterate Chinese.

They crossed into Hunan province, known for its extremely rich farming land and one day to achieve fame on account of its being the birthplace of Mao Zedong. Here, the combination of over-population, land shortage and landlordism over many years had already helped to create the conditions favouring revolution.

At Yongshun, a halt was called and the marchers had a chance to rest and recover in clean surroundings. For eight days they occupied mission premises which the American Catholics and the Finnish Protestants had evidently had to vacate in a hurry.

The soldiers helped themselves freely to the goods left behind. But they allowed Alfred and Arnolis to enjoy some rare treats too: books and magazines in English; tinned milk and tomatoes, butter and Bovril. The missionaries felt sure that their colleagues would not begrudge them these items. They were also able to buy eggs and fruit. With good food and rest, their strength began to return. And there was even treatment, by a man from the Red Cross, for their tired and tender feet.

Other prisoners were put with them for longer or shorter periods. One was from a wealthy family by the name of Liao, who had already paid 7,000 dollars but been told to bring more. Nicknamed 'Fatty Liao' by the soldiers because he was somewhat obese, this young man was very despondent. Even the arrival of a relative to continue negotiations for his release didn't cheer him up. It was as though he sensed that his fate was already sealed.

Meanwhile, like the other prisoners, he was questioned in the room adjoining the one assigned to the missionaries. From this place could be heard the raised, angry voices of the interrogators, and the cries, shouts, screams of their terrified, tortured victims; also the clink of coins as fines were paid by go-betweens who had managed the considerable feat of catching up with the army, having survived bandits and other hazards en route.

News came that the Nationalists were nearby. Reluctantly, the army and its prisoners moved on. The next days and nights were a confusion of stops and starts, ending in a battle won by the Communists. Afterwards, the victors marched back in triumph towards Yongshun, with large numbers of prisoners in tow.

Troops and prisoners billeted just outside the city. Cold and hungry, Alfred and Arnolis remembered that they had a few odd items of food: a tin of unsweetened cream, some butter and a little sugar. From these they mixed their own version of ice cream, which staved off the worst pangs of hunger.

In the morning the army went back into the city for a day and then proceeded, by very long stages, to Dayong, arriving on a Sunday. Roped with the other prisoners, Alfred and Arnolis were taken across the river by ferry and then through the streets.

During their short stay there the two missionaries were given long Chinese gowns, plundered from wealthy Chinese. Among the other prisoners with them was a seventy-year-old former magistrate, a Chinese gentleman of the old school. Alfred and Arnolis spoke to him of their faith. Two months later he was executed.

Late one night the missionaries were suddenly transferred back to the care of the Sixth Army under Xiao Ke. Their new sleeping quarters were in a draughty corridor. Here they were expected to bed down with only two layers of newspapers between them and the hard stone floors. At one end of the passage there was a prisoner cruelly lashed to a chair, in agony and unable to move. Other prisoners were held nearby.

Morning came but there was no breakfast, nor any lunch at noon. Afterwards marching orders were issued. Alfred and Arnolis, along with other prisoners including some elderly folk, women and children, were roped together and escorted through the streets and out of the city.

That night they were put in a granary, five foot by ten, which they shared with two Chinese men. A bar across the room meant that they all had to sleep in cramped positions. One of their room-mates, a man in his eighties, was very agitated and confused. The guards' response was to beat him.

In an adjacent room other prisoners were lying with their hands tied tightly behind their backs, forbidden to move or talk. Those who protested or cried for mercy were beaten. Their food consisted of two small helpings of rice porridge a day, and they had no facilities for washing, so their bloodstained faces bore a continuing testimony to their ill-treatment.

Unable to sleep, Alfred prayed for 'the peace of God in the midst of violence, derangement and hunger. It was like hell, the cries of the tortured most distressing.'

Suddenly one day the guards rushed in to say that an aeroplane had flown over the camp. Alfred and Arnolis pricked up their ears, wondering if they were about to be rescued. Soon afterwards they were ordered to write letters to their wives, the mission and their consuls, urging them to attend to the Red Army's demands. They obeyed and, after being meticulously scrutinised, their letters were given the official stamp of approval by 'The Chinese Soviet Republic National Ratification Department, Chinese Workers' and Farmers'

Red Army, Sixth Battalion Division'. Only then were they allowed to be sent off.

Alfred wrote to Rose:

'We have again been requested to write you to press the ransom for our release. We have been here over a week at this base and our great desire is that someone will be able to come to us while we are still here. We long for news of you and our Guizhou fellow-workers. You will be glad to know that Arnolis and I are both well in health and are treated as well as can be expected under the circumstances...

'My thoughts are continually with you and of course I long for the *revoir* which will be granted in answer to prayer. In the meantime do what you can to send someone. My love to all my friends, with all the love of my heart.'

By the time Rose received this letter, just before Christmas, a great deal had happened to the captives. With relief, first of all, they left the place which they had come to associate with so much evil, cruelty and suffering.

A few days later they arrived in the fertile rice-growing district of Taoyuan. Here they were to stay for some months – and to face their biggest trials yet.

DESPERATE ESCAPE

They stayed in a compound built around a large courtyard. Here there was plenty of room for the guards to exercise and drill, as well as to enjoy times of recreation. Alfred and Arnolis had space too: a sizeable room to themselves, with a bed-frame large enough to allow them to stretch out full-length, kept off the mud floor by stones and criss-crossed with woven ropes. The provision of straw, to lay on top of the ropes, was a touch of luxury.

In these better surroundings they were able to rest and recover. But as Christmas approached they thought longingly of their loved ones. And having as yet no inkling of what was being done on their behalf, they began to dream of escape.

In fact, the mission authorities had been far from idle. Their first priority had been to find the right person to establish communications and begin negotiations with the generals holding the missionaries captive. Hermann Becker, of the Liebenzeller Mission, an associate of CIM, had looked like the ideal choice, having worked in Hunan and met General He Long. Furthermore, the General's nephew owed his life to a mission doctor.

After agreeing to undertake the work, Hermann had lost no time in penning a letter to He Long, referring to their friendship and to the help the mission had given him, and asking him to use his influence with Xiao Ke to release the prisoners. This, along with personal letters from Rose and Rhoda to their husbands, and some food and clothing, he had entrusted to the two courageous Chinese Christians who volunteered to act as messengers.

Mr Yang and Mr Zhai had set off on November 27th. All had gone well at first, but then they had been attacked and robbed of everything by brigands and been forced to return home empty-handed. Mr Becker had immediately set about a second attempt to reach the Red Army. His determined, selfless efforts in the coming months, along with the prayers, help and donations of Chinese Christians, missionary colleagues worldwide and friends and families back home, would only be fully known much later.

In their room in Taoyuan, Alfred and Arnolis began to wonder whether their dream of Christmas with their families could be turned into reality. There was no proper back door to their room. This, along with every other available door, had as usual been removed by the comrades and used by them as beds for the duration. The piece of wood which now served as a makeshift door to the missionaries' room had been somewhat haphazardly hammered into place. Loosening the nails, they decided, would not prove difficult.

Two other things seemed in their favour. Their guard sometimes slipped out and left them on their own for a while. And every evening the soldiers gathered for roll call, followed by a time of Communist-style 'fellowship', when the soldiers listened to pep-talks and sang Party songs, all with catchy tunes but some violent in tone.

'If we're caught it may be execution,' Alfred said.

'It may come to that anyhow,' Arnolis replied.

They wrestled with the inevitable doubts and questions. If they went, should they go together or separately? Were they fit and well enough even to make the attempt? The journey would be long and fraught with dangers – if the cold and the mountainous terrain didn't defeat them, there was the ever-present threat of encountering other troops of Communist soldiers.

In the end, the longing to be free outweighed everything else. They kept working at the door-nails and waiting for the right moment. It came, or so they felt, on a cold moonlit evening in

December – the 17th. Their guard was absent, warming himself at the fire in another room.

They slipped out through their doctored back door, taking some money, the New Testament and *Daily Light*, their bowls and chopsticks. After scaling a wall, they struck out in what they hoped was a westerly direction, every step taking them further away from the sounds of the soldiers singing. In their joy at being free, they kept going for most of the night, avoiding main roads.

Then the sickening truth struck them. Instead of pursuing a more or less straight line, they had somehow curved back on themselves to end up not far from where they had started.

Exhausted and dispirited, they sat and shivered in a drizzle of rain, waiting for the dawn. By its light they saw a house which, greatly daring, they approached. Its occupants stared in fear and disbelief at them, but gave them breakfast before urging them to leave, fearing the imminent arrival of the Red Army.

After walking for some time, the men called at another house. The owners were very hospitable, refusing payment for the food, but too scared to offer shelter. One of them, however, did escort the visitors to a Buddhist temple where it was thought they might receive help.

The place was barricaded like a fortress but a priest heard them attempting to enter, and invited them inside – though only for a moment.

'The soldiers will be here tonight looking for landowners in hiding,' he told them. Then he gave them rice and vegetables and pointed out the direction he thought they should take.

As it was broad daylight, the missionaries dared not travel. Instead they found a secluded spot where, the ground being too wet for sitting or lying on, they paced up and down, praying.

Before dark they set off again, only to discover at dawn that they had again walked in a circle, and were now within a few miles of the Red Army. It was a very low moment. Could God really be helping them, they wondered.

The continuing kindness and generosity of the people they met cheered them somewhat, and afterwards they found a cave in which they felt safe enough to sleep for a while. Setting off from there while it was still light so as to avoid doubling back on themselves again, they kept to the hills, which they felt would be safer.

'God is with us,' they reminded each other.

A woman was carrying buckets to a well. At the sight of the missionaries she scuttled back into her house. A moment later a man emerged from it, and came towards them with a smile of recognition. This was the relative who had attempted to negotiate for the release of 'fatty Liao'. He had every sympathy with Alfred and Arnolis, and invited them in for a meal with his family. But the escapees were soon on their way again.

'As wanted men, we can't really expect hospitality,' said Arnolis. Alfred put it somewhat more wryly later: 'At no time in our lives had we been so wanted, but in our dismal situation we felt neither desired nor desirable, showing unmistakeable symptoms of extreme weariness.'

It was at this low point that they met someone who was more than ready to betray them.

Assured by a woman that there were no Communist soldiers in the valley, the men risked going downhill and calling at a farmhouse. There they were able to buy some straw sandals. But the farmer recognised them and saw a chance of claiming the 500 dollar reward for their safe recapture. So as soon as they had gone, he sent a messenger to tip off the Red Army as to the whereabouts of their escaped prisoners.

Then he ran out and shouted after Alfred and Arnolis, now plodding wearily uphill, 'Stop! There are soldiers at the top of the hill. Come and stay with us till it's dark.' The missionaries hesitated. This was the first person who had offered them shelter. Could they trust him? They were none too sure that they could. But they were tired, and the man persisted.

Once back at the farmhouse, their suspicions came to the fore again. The welcome they were being given seemed false, overdone. They left and began ascending the hill again. But it was too late.

When they were only partway up, they turned and saw that they were being pursued by men waving spears. Arnolis, who accepted that the game was up, was recaptured first. Alfred, who tried to make a last desperate dash for freedom, was overtaken and overpowered shortly afterwards.

Soon back in the camp, the missionaries were very much in disgrace. The captain of the guard showed his anger by slapping them across their faces. Judge Wu, equally furious, gave orders that they should be taken to prison with the other criminals and put in separate cells from one another.

Later they were brought before General Xiao Ke and other officials for questioning.

'Why did you run away?' the Judge asked.

Alfred countered this seemingly unnecessary question with another, not intended rudely: 'In my place wouldn't you have done the same?'

'You're a follower of Jesus,' the Judge retorted. 'And he says if a man slaps you on one cheek, to turn the other; and if a man asks you to go a mile with him, to go two miles with him. And yet you've run away. Now I am not a disciple of Jesus, I am a follower of Marx.'

It was a masterly reply, simultaneously putting the onus squarely back on Alfred and wrongfooting him for failing to live up to his own Christian standards.

Alfred was to comment later that these few verses from the Sermon on the Mount were constantly quoted by the Communists, to the exclusion of everything else Jesus had ever said. On this occasion used to induce self-condemnation, the words normally formed part of the Communists' indictment against Jesus and his followers, for, as revolutionaries, they were diametrically opposed to such non-resistance.

The Judge also questioned the missionaries as to who had

helped them during their escape. But on this matter the two men remained silent.

The interrogation over, Alfred and Arnolis were transferred to a room where they were kept closely guarded. At night their hands were tied behind their backs and their feet roped together. They slept at opposite corners, on the hard wooden floor, with nothing but straw and bricks by way of bed and bedding. Forbidden to talk to one another, they could only address the guards in the prescribed manner, relying on them for everything and at the mercy of their whims.

'Comrade, I want to make an announcement.'

'What do you want to announce?'

'Please may I turn over?'

'No.'

Sometimes the answer might be 'yes'. But in turning over, the prisoners could hardly fail to dislodge their straw 'blanket'. Sooner or later, a guard might or might not come across and cover them. Their responses were unpredictable. On one occasion, a guard left Arnolis uncovered and shivering for a long time; on another, a different man took the trouble to loosen the ropes binding Alfred.

There was little to do but pray and think, with pain, of loved ones and happier times. Alfred visualised the bustle and colour of the streets of Manchester: the shops bulging with Christmas food and gifts; the strains of much-loved and familiar Christmas carols mingling with the happy talk and laughter.

Before all this and the miscarriage, he and Rose had been looking forward to an extra special Christmas – one in which they had been expecting to celebrate also the birth of their own newborn baby. Instead, he and Arnolis had to face the grim ordeal of a Communist-style trial.

The officials told them: 'Answer with care if you want to win the crowd's favour and get a lighter sentence.' Alfred found the injunction disturbing. 'How can we do that?' he wondered. 'How will we know what to say?'

Then he remembered a promise of Jesus to his followers: 'And when they bring you before the synagogue, and the rulers, and the authorities, be not anxious how or what ye shall answer, or what ye shall say; for the Holy Spirit shall teach you in that very hour what ye ought to say.'

His anxiety evaporated. God was with him; he would show him what to say.

ON TRIAL

The trial took place on Christmas Eve, in the marketplace. The chief judge and his two assistants sat on three intricately carved chairs placed on a specially erected and gaily decorated stage. The prisoners were brought in one by one and made to sit at the front of the stage facing the crowds.

The first prisoner was Chinese. His accusation was that he had hidden landowners in return for money. The judges questioned him. Then the crowd were asked for their verdict.

'Sha!' ('Kill!') they shouted. The terrified man attempted to speak but it was no use. He was taken away to be executed.

The next prisoners in the dock were the missionaries – first Arnolis, then Alfred.

Alfred was asked to give his full name in English and then to spell it. As he did this, the crowd roared with laughter. Arnolis had had the same reaction when, complying with instructions, he had spoken a few words in Miao, a tribal language of which he could speak a little. Amid the taunting, Alfred kept reminding himself of the promise that had helped him earlier.

The missionaries were questioned about their background. In replying, Alfred stressed that he had Swiss nationality and that Switzerland was the oldest republic in the world and had no unequal treaties with China.

His activities in China then came under scrutiny. 'Why did you come to China?' he was asked.

'To tell you of the one true God and to call you to repentance,' he replied. Not wishing to pursue this, the judge changed the subject.

Arnolis was asked, 'What have you got to say about the aggression of the imperialistic countries in China, such as the Opium War, foreign gunboats in Chinese rivers and unequal treaties?'

He replied, 'I feel ashamed that Britain forced the opium on China and unequal treaties are, of course, unfair.' This response was greeted with approval.

Finally, the chief judge called on the people for their verdict. Astonishingly, his appeal met with silence. Alfred was suddenly reminded of the story of Daniel in the lions' den.

Then a single voice shouted, 'Sha!' and another, 'Da!' ('Beat!'). Hurriedly, the judge rose and ordered the missionaries to retire. A little later they were summoned back to hear the judgment. It was read out from a long document, obviously prepared in advance of the trial.

It began: 'Second record of judgment issued by the Chinese Soviet United Realms of Judicial Commission of the Provinces Hunan, Hubei, Sichuan and Guizhou'. Both defendants, it claimed, had been 'sent to China under imperialistic principles to delude with the teaching of Jesus the docile people' and had then explored the country 'as a vanguard in the interests of imperialism with a view to dividing up China like a melon'. Specific allegations related to their having photographed strategic places; worn Chinese clothes and spoken the language of the people as a front for their under-cover activities; preached Christ's doctrine of non-resistance; attempted to escape from prison.

Presumed guilty, sentences were pronounced. The fine was to be increased by 150,000 dollars. Arnolis was to be imprisoned for one year and Alfred for a year and six months – his longer sentence reflecting the fact that he had instigated the escape, resisted recapture and then – or so they falsely alleged – struck one of his captors with a stick.

Other prisoners were brought for trial. They, like the first man tried, were all sentenced to death and executed.

Once again, Alfred and Arnolis had escaped death. But they were kept closely guarded and frequently summoned for more interrogations.

'Your attempted escape led to the execution of your guard,' Alfred was told. This merited punishment. But he was to be allowed to choose one out of the three suggested penalties of carrying a hundred loads of water a day, receiving daily beatings of a hundred stripes, or only being allowed to sleep for two out of every twenty-four hours.

As all these would have been well beyond his strength, Alfred declined to make a choice between them. Instead he offered to do anything his captors could think of that did lie within his capabilities. But no suggestions were forthcoming, and the supposedly executed guard was spotted alive and well. Evidently, the Communists had been out to induce guilt and fear in the missionaries, as one way of punishing them for having had the effrontery to try and escape.

Officially there was still no conversation allowed between the missionaries. But they managed to mouth words at one another when the guards weren't looking. And Alfred taught Arnolis the rudiments of sign language. Catching them communicating in this way, the soldiers were suspicious.

'What devilry are you up to?' they demanded.

Christmas morning came, bringing tantalising memories of warm fires and festive rooms; feelings of joy and loving closeness; bright colours and cheerful sounds; the smell and taste of roasting turkey.

By contrast, the missionaries faced a grim and cheerless prospect. No fire, although it was very cold; nothing to do all day except sit in their separate corners. Meals, it's true, would be served – probably rice and vegetables, as usual. But only to be eaten in silence.

Alfred sat in his corner, sunk in gloom. And then everything changed.

The message of Christmas suddenly crystallised with the sudden entrance into his heart and mind of the one word: 'Emmanuel'. It was a shaft of light; a burst of joy.

Somehow he must share the message with Arnolis. Surreptitiously, he gathered some straw and began forming it into letters on the floor: E-M-M-A-N-U-E-L. The guard was unaware of what was going on. But Arnolis understood, and was flooded by the same transforming hope.

The missionaries were summoned again, this time to be told that their strict imprisonment would be lifted if they could pay a dollar a day to cover the period of their sentence.

'But we have no money,' said Alfred. On the assumption that they would eventually pay, they were to be allowed to speak to one another – but only in Chinese.

Once again they wrote letters as directed, this time with the proviso that if two anti-aircraft guns were donated, the fine would be reduced considerably.

'Speak to me, God. Give me a word for today,' Alfred prayed. It was New Year's Day and his thirty-eighth birthday. He longed for something special to mark the occasion.

'O, rest in the Lord. Wait patiently for him, and he shall give thee thy heart's desires. Commit thy way unto him and trust in him. Fret not thyself because of evil doers. O, rest in the Lord.' The words burst into silent song inside his head, courtesy of Mendelssohn's *Elijah,* and became his word from God. He was to wait *patiently*, the adverb hinting that the time of waiting might not be short.

As prisoners everywhere are wont to do, Arnolis and Alfred wrote the date on the wall of their room. AD 1935. The guards understood the figures, but what did the letters mean, they wanted to know. The missionaries were not slow to enlighten them in the matter of *anno domini* – 'the year of our Lord'.

In the evening a feast of fat pork was enjoyed by all. Not long afterwards Alfred and Arnolis were transferred to another room. They shared this with two other prisoners. One was an elderly man. His home was nearby and his son often sent extra food for him, but this rarely reached him. Once when it did, the old gentleman received it with true old-style Chinese courtesy, by giving a low bow to the official concerned.

The man responded by clouting and reprimanding the old fellow. Bowing was anti-Communist – he was told sternly – part of the old class system that had been done away with.

That, at any rate, was Communist theory. In practice, as Alfred and others observed, a class hierarchy still existed, albeit a different one. Peasants and soldiers were now at the top, with artisans on the next rung and small-businessmen – a necessary nuisance – under them. Finally, right at the bottom came religious teachers, who were regarded as non-productive and hence denied all rights.

At the same time, respect for old age and politeness, once cardinal virtues, cut no ice whatever in the Communist scheme of things. Having received this message loud and clear, the old man did his best to learn and abide by the new rules and so to curry favour with the authorities. Told that his traditional long finger-nails were old-fashioned and unhygienic, he promptly cut them short.

He was an opium smoker and, as a special concession during the New Year period, the officials allowed him to have some opium brought to him from his home. Along with gambling, opium smoking was not officially allowed among the soldiers – although the drug was certainly seized and used as currency by the Red Army – so any addicts who wanted to enlist had to go on a programme to get themselves off it. But old habits die hard, and a few of the guards begged the old man for a secret smoke.

It struck Alfred and Arnolis again that they were receiving better treatment than were the other prisoners. Other recaptured escapees were beaten mercilessly by one guard after another. Some prisoners were tortured and practically starved.

Many died, but in death as in life they were treated with no respect.

Two women came to beg for the release of a very elderly relative. To their horror, they saw his dead body tied to a pole and being carried out like a pig to market. When they asked if they could give their deceased loved one a decent burial, the captain of the guard refused, adding callously, 'What thing is he to you?' Almost daily for a time, men and women were taken away to be executed, the men stripped to the waist and tightly bound.

'Seeing all this,' Alfred wrote, 'we felt how much our Lord was restraining the guards in their attitude towards us.'

GOOD NEWS, BAD NEWS

From the window of their room, Alfred and Arnolis watched the guards enjoying their periods of recreation. They organised impromptu concerts or played party games, such as 'drop the handkerchief' or 'pig and whistle'. Their enjoyment was noisy and wholehearted, often expressed in hand-clapping and uproarious laughter, especially when anyone made a mistake or was caught out. More skilled games or activities included basketball, wrestling, sword-dancing and fencing with bayonets.

Alfred longed for some activity to enliven the tedium of his long days and nights. Unexpectedly, a Chinese prisoner who shared their room for a time unwittingly showed him the way to achieve this. He was unravelling a pair of socks. Alfred went across to help him, and asked what he planned to do with the wool.

'I want to make "ears" to go inside my sandals,' the man replied.

Alfred was suddenly reminded of an incident in his childhood. While recovering from an illness, and presumably feeling bored, he had been taught to crochet by his mother. Now he kept thinking that if only he could get hold of some wool and a crochet hook, and remember what to do – he'd be able to make things.

The wool came first – a gift from a prisoner, who was released before he'd had time to make his unravelled wool into 'ears'. Then the crochet hook: a chopstick which Alfred whittled into the required shape using a sword borrowed from one of the guards. Finally, as he started to wind the wool round the hook, the memory of what he had been taught so long ago returned. And so began Alfred's new career as a maker of woollen garments.

To the guards' manifest astonishment, he proceeded to crochet a pair of bedsocks for Arnolis – a great comfort since neither of the missionaries had shoes. Very impressed, the guards then brought Alfred more wool and asked him to make a cap for the company trumpeter.

From then on he was kept very busy making caps, gloves, mittens, belts and jerseys to order. He even attempted a mosquito net to discourage as many insects as possible from sharing their sleeping quarters. Arnolis helped with the unravelling and wool-winding. Alfred's repertory was strictly limited to chain-stitch and his finished garments sometimes ended up looking rather unusual if not bizarre. But no one seemed to mind and Alfred was delighted at having something useful to do.

The guards, of course, thoroughly approved of their prisoner's industry. One thing they did not approve of, however, was the missionaries' practice of saying grace before meals. This smacked to them of superstition, or 'devilry', as they put it. But Alfred and Arnolis kept patiently explaining what they were doing and, in the end, the guards never actually made them stop giving thanks, despite threatening to do so.

The Communists were similarly suspicious and scornful of the missionaries' observance of Sunday as a day of rest and prayer. But again they allowed it to continue. For quite different reasons, the Red Army soldiers also made Sunday a different day from the rest of the week; one in which they would do odd jobs, such as cleaning their guns, instead of drilling.

With something to do, time hung less heavily on Alfred's hands. But release was still a constant theme in his and Arnolis' thoughts. Was anyone doing anything about it?

Arnolis' bed being near a partition, he could often hear what was being said in the other room. One day in February, he heard the judge addressing some persons unseen as 'the running dogs of the foreigners'. That, surely, could only mean one thing. Controlling his excitement, he turned to Alfred and said, 'I think someone has come to find us.'

He was right. Three exhausted messengers had arrived from Mr Becker, after fifteen days of running the gauntlet of bandits and soldiers, sometimes passing skeletons and beheaded bodies. On arrival, Mr Zhai, Mr Yang and Mr He delivered Mr Becker's letter to General He Long and the following joint letter from Rhoda and Rose to both generals.

Dear Sirs,
'We have not hitherto communicated with yourself or other officers, as it seemed to us scarcely fitting for foreign women to write to you, but in view of the special circumstances we feel that we must send this letter to you.

'It is with no other reason than to do good and to show kindness to the Chinese people, especially the poor, that we have come to China. Neither have we at any time acted in any way adversely to the interests of any class of people, our hope being to show kindness to all at all times.

'It is now more than three months since General Xiao Ke came to Jiuzhou in the course of the military operations and took us captive. We are grateful that he was willing at that time to let us and the children go free. We are very pleased also that our husbands, Messrs Hayman and Bosshardt, have stated in their letters more than once that they have had kindly treatment and consideration during the time of their captivity. But we would remind you that for months their wives have waited anxiously for their release, and Mr Hayman has four sons who are grieved and sorry that they have not been able to see their father whom they expected to meet at New Year season.

'We are not in a position to demand that they should be set free, neither is it in our power to make any promises of ransom or reward, but we would appeal to your kindness and generosity, who also are fathers, that for the sake of the women and children who have long been separated from their loved ones that you will give orders to your officers to release our loved ones at once and let them return to us. And we shall invoke a blessing on you and kindness in return for this shown to us.'

On the day following their interview with the generals, the messengers were allowed to speak with the missionaries for an hour.

'Our world was suddenly a place of extraordinary beauty,' Alfred wrote, for the three men brought them wonderful news. Rose, Rhoda and the children were safe and well, and Grace Emblen had indeed been released and was fine.

The three Chinese messengers made light of the hazards of their journey, but Alfred and Arnolis were in no doubt that they had risked their lives and thanked them with all their hearts, aware of the inadequacy of mere words in such a situation.

At the end of their time together, having noticed that Alfred and Arnolis were barefoot, the Chinese men took off their shoes and socks and handed them over to the two missionaries. 'We had steeled ourselves against hardship,' Alfred was to write later, 'but against such an act of friendship, we had no defences.'

Evidently the Communist leaders had plenty of defences against the appeals made to them by Hermann Becker and the prisoners' wives.

'You must not put any hope in our former friendship with Mr Becker,' General He Long told them, 'as under the new regime all friendships and even home ties are secondary to Communist principles.'

The letter which was sent back to the mission was very much in keeping with his tone and words. It demanded the delivery, by March 15th of anti-aircraft guns, and, by April 14th, of 100,000 dollars and a whole range of medicines. Otherwise, the death sentence would be carried out on the two captives.

The missionaries were transferred to a dark, gloomy room with boarded-up windows. But they had a good Chinese bed, a stone brazier and a cupboard; and, instead of a succession of different guards, they now had four who were specially assigned to them. Also, at first they were allowed to go into the much lighter, adjoining room, belonging to the captain of the guard. Here they could see to read and, in Alfred's case, crochet. Then one day they were told, without explanation, that they would have to stay in their own room all the time.

'But I have much work to do and our room is too dark,' Alfred protested.

'Then you must give up your work,' the captain replied.

Disconsolately, the missionaries returned to their room. The secretary followed with a kettle of tea – a gesture of sympathy.

In the weeks which followed, they spent many hours each day praying and reciting all the Bible verses and hymns they could remember. Together, they totalled about 500. Sometimes they would group the hymns and verses under themes or try some other similar exercise that helped them to remember, dwell on and be refreshed by the spiritual realities of God's love and power, his presence and promises.

Each day, through a crack in the roof, one small ray of sunshine would penetrate into their gloomy, shuttered room, and make a circular pattern of light on one of its walls. By noting the position of the circle, they were able to estimate the hours between 11 a.m. and 3 p.m.

From the next door room, to which they were now forbidden access, they could hear new recruits being interviewed. After establishing the interviewee's name and age and whether or not he or she was illiterate or smoked opium, the questions and answers would follow the same pattern with minor variations.

'Why do you want to become a Red Soldier?'

'Because we do not have enough to eat at home.'

'Do you have any debts?'

'Yes.'

'Don't pay them. Are you willing to fight against landowners, to give information against them, and concerning any oppression of the poor?'

'Yes.'

During March, the sixth month of captivity, reports reached the mission to say that Alfred and Arnolis had been executed. The news seemed reliable so Mr Warren, at headquarters, felt he had no option but to pass it on to Rhoda in Shanghai and Rose now in Zhenjiang. For a whole weekend, the women were numb with anguish, believing themselves to be widows.

On the Monday fresh news arrived, seeming to contradict the earlier reports. This was confirmed when Mr Becker's messengers returned to say they had talked for one hour with Arnolis and Alfred. So Rose and Rhoda dared to hope again. They were to receive many similar jolts to their emotions in the coming months. But their trust in God remained firm, and was an inspiration to those around them.

Towards the end of the month, severe food shortage forced the Red Army to leave Taoyuan. The propaganda squad plastered the premises with slogans, so that the incoming government troops would be challenged, as fellow peasants and artisans, to desert and join the Communists – something which many of them were, in any case, doing, and would continue to do.

Well before dawn one morning, the long column slipped stealthily away, taking their accumulated possessions. Alfred's haversack contained his bowl, chopsticks, toothbrush. A porter carried the rest of his things – travelling rug, flannelette sheet, patchwork quilt, wadded coverlet, extra clothing and shoes.

After a few days they pitched camp, just outside a small market town. The propaganda squad got busy at once. As there were no suitable premises for their purposes, they built a place out of straw mats, evergreen branches and bamboo poles, which they turned into a reading room and library filled with Communist leaflets, books and posters.

IN EXTREMITY

Alfred and Arnolis were again assigned to a granary. It was so small that their bed could only fit in diagonally. Of the two remaining corners, one was boarded up, but the other afforded them a great treat after their weeks of enforced 'hibernation' – letting in light and giving them a view, beyond the courtyard, of the lush green countryside.

But the prospect in other ways was not so encouraging. After five days they were issued with an ultimatum: 'You must pay the fine within the next month – and if it is not paid by May 9th, you will receive the extreme penalty.' This had the ring of a firm, official ultimatum, and the missionaries heard it with quaking hearts, even as they responded with the customary polite smiles.

They were ordered to spell out the new terms to Mr Becker, adding that he must also give twenty dollars to the courier, a man named Mr Ding whom the Communists had found willing to act as messenger.

The next day they were on the move again. Now, for the first time, they were told that they would have to manage without a porter. They 'wore' their rugs and took turns in carrying their other things made up into a large bundle.

By the end of the day, Alfred was showing symptoms of serious illness. Exhaustion, stomach upsets, aching limbs – all these he'd experienced before. But the degree of breathlessness and weakness he now felt was something new, as was his chest pain.

'I'm going to faint,' he gasped – and almost did.

The guards were alarmed by his appearance and relieved him of his bundle. But over the next days his condition worsened and he kept collapsing. Forced to keep going while his body was wracked with pain and crying out for rest, he slipped deeper and deeper into despair until finally, for the first time, he felt he could take no more.

'Shoot me! Shoot me!' he cried out wildly to the captain of the guard.

'My endurance,' Alfred was to write later, 'had gone. With only a month to go, I might as well die a little earlier. Rose and my family would understand that living had reached an unbearable pitch.'

His uncharacteristic outburst had the effect of making the guards modify their behaviour somewhat. But their job was still to keep the prisoners moving with the rest of the column.

Alfred collapsed again. This time the guards dragged him into a field and left him there. Totally prostrated but still conscious, he heard them return some time later to bend over him and verify to one another that he was alive and still breathing.

A stretcher was improvised and two porters were assigned to carry it. But by that time Alfred had got up and was managing to stagger along. Eventually, he caught up with Arnolis and the other members of their party, resting after a meal of cold rice.

Having swallowed a little of the same fare, Alfred lay down in the attic room to which he'd been assigned. All he wanted was to be allowed to stay there undisturbed for a very long time. But it was not to be. There was news that the Red Army was routing the Nationalists at a place not far away and the soldiers were ordered to go and help their colleagues there immediately.

Alfred was given a horse to ride most of the time, but the journey proved a nightmare nonetheless. He developed a high fever and the chest pains increased. When they arrived at Sangzhi, Arnolis tried massage to see if this would bring his colleague some relief. The guards finally became alarmed and asked Alfred if there was anything he felt he would like to eat. He had a mental picture of some ripe pumeloes which he'd recently seen in a street stall bordering their route. But for some reason the guards were unable to procure these. Instead they brought large, succulent oranges, and some sweetmeats and dumplings. Alfred ate what he could, relishing the change from the mouldy rice that they had recently been reduced to.

Meanwhile Mr Becker had sent out several more negotiators, but none of them had succeeded in reaching their destination. Then on April 19th, Mr Ding had reached him with news of the ultimatum. Two days later he bravely returned to deliver the message that the Communists' demands were impossible. For Alfred and Arnolis he brought some printed material from the mission. It included an account of the execution of John and Betty Stam, which made very sombre reading for the two captives.

Two months after the capture of the Bosshardts and Haymans, the missionary couple and their tiny baby, Helen Priscilla, had been seized by Communists in Jingde, Anhui, and later condemned to death as imperialist spies. A Chinese man had pleaded for little Helen to be spared. 'Your life or hers' – he had been told, just before they had killed him.

The next day John and Betty had been led away, bound, barefoot and stripped of some of their outer clothing. A Christian medicine-seller had fallen on his knees and pleaded for them. His execution had preceded theirs. The baby and the beheaded bodies of her parents had been found by an evangelist some thirty-six hours later. Helen Priscilla, whom he had managed to smuggle to a mission home, was now safe and being well cared for.

News of the Communist ultimatum against Alfred and Arnolis drove friends and supporters to pray as perhaps never before. Union Hall, Manchester, among other churches, convened a special meeting on the eve of the date set for the execution.

A *Daily Mail* reporter present at this subsequently wrote in his column: 'To pay any part of the sum demanded would be a potential source of income to bandits. The mission dare not take this risk. It is hoped that the bandits' threat to murder the captives was bluff ... One after another members of the congregation stood up to speak. The remainder sat with bowed heads, people of all ages drawn together by a common bond – their belief in God and their love for Mr Bosshardt. Occasionally a muffled sob broke out. Men's voices quivered, women found their eyes suddenly obscured by tears.'

It was an especially agonising time for the two families. Yet Alfred's mother was to say, 'Neither I nor my son's wife ever favoured ransoming him. To have done that would have put dozens of missionaries in China to great peril.'

While around the world people prayed, on May 9th the judge sent for Alfred and Arnolis. He said, 'We realise that Shanghai is far from here and maybe your wives have not yet had time to get the money to us. We extend the time to May 30th.'

Gladly, the missionaries wrote letters conveying this reprieve. In the meantime, before these arrived, family and friends were in agony, torn between hope and fear, while holding on to God and his promises.

After much scrambling up hillsides and fording of streams the army reached Zhongbao, just across the border into Hubei, where the Nationalists had been routed. During the ensuing celebrations General He Long mounted a platform to make a speech. His oratory and charismatic personality, handsome physique and striking black moustache, combined to ensure that he had everyone's undivided attention.

Suddenly he turned to address the missionaries. 'Unless you pay the fine quickly, we will chop off your heads,' he shouted, striking the flat of his hand against the back of his neck to make his meaning doubly clear. 'Don't think your beards will save you,' he continued. 'I killed a foreigner with a beard many times longer than yours.'

The allusion to the long Chinese tradition of associating beards with honour was meaningless, since Alfred and Arnolis were unshaven not by choice but through lack of the necessary facilities. Washing, shaving and hair-cutting were rare luxuries in their way of life.

Having threatened the missionaries, the General proceeded to denounce them as spies. The newly captured Nationalist general, named Zhang, and his two majors, were similarly branded.

In any lulls that occurred between marches and other bursts of activity, Alfred continued to ply his crochet hook. One Sunday, Assistant Judge Liu came to ask how the prisoner was getting on with a garment he was making for him. When he was told that the missionary didn't work on a Sunday, he became angry.

'Very well, if you insist, I will finish your garment,' said Alfred, and reluctantly proceeded to do so. But, as things turned out, Mr Liu got very little joy out of the finished article. On the first day after receiving it he ordered a Chinese prisoner to carry his clothes. But the man in question absconded soon afterwards, taking the Judge's precious new garment with him.

By May 30th no money had been received from Mr Becker, but the Red Army had other things on its mind. The soldiers were attempting to besiege a city while trying to avoid being hit by bombs dropped from Nationalist aircraft. While the fighting was going on, the prisoners and their guards took cover in nearby caves. Alfred was grateful for the chance to rest. His toes had festered and he made a poultice of hot rice to ease the pain and reduce the swelling.

Throughout the summer Mr Becker kept trying to locate, keep abreast of and negotiate with Generals He Long and Xiao Ke. He was now offering 3,000 dollars, not as a ransom payment, but to cover the food and other expenses incurred by the missionaries.

It was Judge Wu again who summoned the missionaries to let them know what the Communists thought of this latest offer.

'Mr Becker is playing games with me, offering only 3,000 dollars for you,' he stormed. 'Why, we require more than that even for a small landowner! Write and tell him to gather as much money as he can and send it quickly. We will give him fifty days to get it here.' After a pause, he amended this to, 'We will give him a little longer – until the end of next month.'

Sensing a slight change in the Judge's attitude, Alfred dared to ask, 'And what will happen if the money does not come by then?'

There was another momentary hesitation and then the Judge said, 'You will be executed – at least one of you will.'

This time, the final version of the letters which the missionaries sent didn't specify a large sum of money or a date. Instead, it merely stated that if the middlemen arrived again without any money at all, they would be treated as spies – which meant they would be imprisoned or even, perhaps, executed.

Alfred and Arnolis felt that all this added up to a less intransigent line and were somewhere relieved.

The messengers came again. Hermann Becker had raised his offer to 6,000 dollars for the missionaries' board. He would deliver the money personally if the Communists chose a safe neutral meeting place and brought the prisoners there, ready for the exchange.

For Alfred and Arnolis there were letters from their wives and one from Alfred's mother to Hermann Becker; also photos – one of Rose, two of Arnolis' children and one of Alfred's parents. Even these personal letters, the Judge ordered, must be translated into Chinese. In her letter, written on the fourth anniversary of her marriage to Alfred, Rose had quoted their wedding hymn.

'Do you wish me to translate the poem?' Alfred asked the Judge.

'Yes, everything,' was the uncompromising reply.

In the end the Judge kept all the letters, but at least the missionaries had their photographs to treasure and keep looking at. The guards saw them too and urged, 'Pay the money quickly and you can be free to see your families.' Their attitude had been growing noticeably softer and kinder towards their prisoners. Some were amazed by the missionaries' spirit of cheerful endurance.

At last the Judge sent for the missionaries and spelt out what they were to write in reply to the letters just received. First, they were to confess they were spies who should never have come to China and for whom, therefore, the heavy fines being demanded were fully justified. Second, they were to add that they had attempted to escape and so further incriminated themselves. Third, they were to make clear that they would be set free when the money was handed over, along with some medicines, duly listed.

Alfred sat down to write the letter but found he could not bring himself to set down the lie that he was a spy. What he wrote instead, although only a minute deviation from instructions, did not escape the Judge's meticulous vetting.

He summoned the missionary and demanded angrily, 'Why do you say "*as* spies"? You *are* spies. So write that you are spies.'

'That is a falsehood – I refuse to write it,' Alfred replied.

Judge Wu started to shout and bluster. 'You *are* a spy. The evidence was there when you were judged. Otherwise why did you come to China?'

'I came to China to preach the gospel.'

'Then why did you have a camera?'

'I had no camera.'

'Why have you bought land in China?'

'We bought no land in China.'

'I command you to write this letter as we say.'

'This letter is to my wife and she knows that I am not a spy even if I am made to write it.'

'I don't care to whom it is written, you must write it according to our wishes or we will execute you immediately.' As he said this, the Judge's expression conveyed sheer hatred.

'You had better do as the Judge wants – he has a very bad temper,' advised the soldier who later escorted Alfred back to his quarters. Reluctantly the missionary complied.

Afterwards he and Arnolis were at last allowed to meet and speak with the messengers. The meeting took place in the Judge's house. On learning that the missionaries no longer had a Bible, one of the men went and got a copy of St John's gospel from his belongings.

But before he could hand this over the Judge took it, saying 'I must inspect it. If it is all right I will pass it on.' That was the last that Alfred and Arnolis saw of it.

Still not satisfied with what the missionaries had written, the Judge wrote the letter himself in Chinese, then made the men translate it into English. It was this stilted effort that the messengers eventually delivered to Mr Becker.

While praying earnestly about these continuing negotiations, the missionaries also took every opportunity to speak of the Christian faith to those around them. Of these, General Zhang, for one, seemed ready to listen and would often ask questions.

Alfred noticed that this Nationalist General was not ridiculed and humiliated by the Communists but rather treated well and with respect. In fact, he was asked to instruct the Red Army soldiers in military tactics.

BEATEN WITH RODS

One evening Alfred and Arnolis were summoned from their beds. Judge Wu, Chairman Liu and other Communist leaders were sitting in a circle. General Zhang was there too.

When the missionaries had sat down on the vacant chairs evidently placed there for them, they were questioned and ridiculed for a time and then Judge Wu said, 'We want you to sing, but I warn you not to sing any of your sacred songs.'

'We've practised nothing but hymns,' said Alfred.

The awkward silence was broken by a petite woman, the wife of one of the leaders, saying, 'O well, sing anything you like.' A moment later, the strains of a resurrection hymn rang out: 'I am he that liveth, that liveth and was dead.'

'Nothing wrong with the harmony,' commented Chairman Liu, in Chinese.

A few months later he was executed as a 'counter-revolutionary'. This was a term used to cover any idea or activity that could be seen to smack of capitalism or anything else that might be classed as anti-communist. During the 1950s there were to be systematic concerted campaigns against counter-revolutionaries but even at this stage denunciations and executions on this basis within the Communist ranks were not uncommon.

In this fraught and dangerous situation, the missionaries took each new day as a gift from God. But some days brought experiences which savagely tested such an attitude.

'Judge Wu wants to see the younger foreigner.' This message

arrived when Alfred and Arnolis were singing the *Te Deum* as part of
a time of worship. Unofficially, they knew that messengers from
Hermann Becker had arrived, but so far they had not been allowed
to speak with them. Perhaps they would now meet them.

They did, but not as they would have wished to. Alfred was
escorted by a young guard to the Judge's house and taken to a room
filled with students. At the front of the room were the messengers,
Mr Ding and Mr Gao, looking very alarmed. Beside them,
dominating the scene, was Judge Wu. He was clearly furious, and
his first question left Alfred in no doubt as to why this was. Once
again, the mission had had the effrontery not to send any money.
The Judge's patience was at an end, and he was about to
demonstrate to the missionaries, messengers and assembled
students the strength of his anger and the extent of his power
and authority.

'Why hasn't the money come?' he demanded.

'I don't know. We're dependent on our friends,' Alfred replied.

'Hit him on the face!' the Judge ordered the guards. The ensuing
blow nearly knocked Alfred off his feet.

'I denounce you as a spy and you are worthy of death,' shouted
the Judge.

'Now,' he continued, addressing himself to the students, 'we will
punish this imperialist like the British punish our poor people in
places like Hong Kong.' Turning back to the guards he barked,
'Strip him.'

Alfred's gown was ripped off him. He felt the shock of cold water
on his back as someone spewed this over him. Then two guards held
his arms. Knowing what was coming, Alfred had a flashing mental
picture of Christ not only beaten but crucified – for him.

He was struck again and again by a length of bamboo, its thinness
and regular notching adding to the pain of each blow. Alfred bowed
his head and focused his thoughts on the crucifixion. As the beating
continued, the agony was almost unbearable.

'If it be possible …' The words of Jesus became a cry from his heart, his presence so real that no sound escaped from his lips. The punishment was not having the desired effect, as far as the Judge was concerned.

'You're not laying it on hard enough,' he shouted. Alfred's body involuntarily writhed and twitched as sharper blows descended on it. Suddenly the Judge stepped down and snatched the bamboo to administer yet more savage 'punishment'.

'When will it end?' was Alfred's anguished thought. Still he did not cry out. At last the assault was over.

'How soon can you get the money?' demanded the Judge.

'It's not within my power to say,' gasped Alfred. 'We've always written the letters you asked.'

The Judge then accused him of secretly sending an uncensored letter from Sangzhi, advising Mr Becker not to pay the fine.

The messengers could not bear to see Alfred suffer any more. 'Name a date,' they urged him. In the end, hazarding a guess based on the information he had as to Hermann Becker's whereabouts, he said, 'Ten days.'

After that he was dismissed and Arnolis was summoned to undergo a similar ordeal and then ordered to write to Mr Becker, giving him a fortnight for the payment of money.

Supper that night was salted fish. The missionaries removed as much of the salt as they could, dissolved it in some hot tea and gently applied this solution, when sufficiently cool, to one another's smarting, bloodstained backs. They sensed the silent sympathy of the young guard who had escorted them to and from their ordeal and held their arms during the beating, and were touched when he brought them some popcorn.

The next day Alfred received an unexpected and quite different bonus.

Judge Wu summoned him. There was an article from the *Hankow News*, an English paper, that he wanted Alfred to translate. As the Judge opened the paper, Alfred's eye fell on a heading: 'The Word of God'. Below that was a verse which he quickly read and assimilated: 'Cast thy burden on the Lord and he will sustain thee. He will not suffer the righteous to be moved.' The words were a shot in the arm. Alfred could hardly wait to finish the translation and share the encouragement with Arnolis.

A week later, Alfred and Arnolis were asked to translate Hermann Becker's latest letter. It conveyed something of the dilemma the negotiator found himself in. Should he pay 6,000 dollars and perhaps achieve nothing, or pay 3,000 dollars to test the Communists' integrity and, if they then released a prisoner, follow this with the other 3,000 dollars for the second prisoner?

The response from the Communist officials was stern but also, on the main issue, reassuring. There was to be no bargaining. And for 'military reasons', they insisted, both prisoners would be released or neither: there was no question of only one being set free. The money was to be delivered in Sangzhi, and until it arrived the beatings would continue daily.

The messengers were optimistic about the outcome: Mr Becker would be able to send the money and it would, they felt sure, secure the missionaries' freedom.

Heavy bombardment by government troops soon forced the Communists to retreat back towards Sangzhi. They had to travel through the mountains in intense heat. Thirst was a constant problem. One day local children collected water from a stream in a bucket and offered it to the weary prisoners.

No such compassion was demonstrated by the guards towards an elderly woman who attempted to escape by jumping down a steep slope. Quickly recaptured, she sat gasping for breath while her captors discussed what was to be done. Half a day's travel lay ahead. They could either drag the old lady along or execute her. Casually, the second alternative was agreed on, and three or four young soldiers haggled for the 'honour' of the task. The oldest, aged about twenty, 'won'. He dragged the woman some distance away, wielding a sharp sword which he had borrowed. A second soldier carrying a hoe followed.

Shortly afterwards the two men returned smiling, as though nothing of consequence had happened.

By the time they arrived back in Sangzhi the missionaries were feeling very unwell with gastric problems. They were put in a hot, mosquito-infested room. Fortunately, on visiting this Assistant Magistrate Wang ordered that they should be transferred to better lodgings. But food was a continuing problem.

Unable to eat steamed rice, Arnolis was given gruel – the sometimes sour left-overs from other prisoners' meals. His condition deteriorated. It distressed Alfred to see his friend growing daily more gaunt and thin. At last the guards were sufficiently alarmed to see about getting him better food. But in his state, recovery was bound to be slow.

The negotiators were back with letters, Christian magazines and a devotional book, *Streams in the Desert*, by Mrs Charles E. Cowman. To these joys was added the news that Mr Becker had written to say he was willing to pay 6,000 dollars.

But the Communists' reply, stating that the fine was to be reduced to 10,000 dollars, made clear, in an oblique fashion, that this sum was still not enough.

'Your friends will surely be able to collect such a small amount as 10,000 dollars,' the guards said, encouragingly, and the messengers added their reassurances: 'We'll bring the money as quickly as possible. Mr Becker will be able to get this amount.'

The missionaries dared to hope that their long captivity would soon end. But in their present state of health, and surrounded as they were by the sufferings of others, life was grim indeed.

In the room opposite them was a middle-aged woman who seemed to be suffering from dementia. Maltreated by the guards and unable to look after herself properly, she was a pitiful sight. In another room were crammed twenty prisoners, among them a pregnant woman, who gave birth one night to a stillborn baby.

The missionaries fared better, and their room-mates, Mr Geng and Mr Li, were keen to learn about the Christian faith.

'Perhaps,' Alfred reflected later, 'they saw something of the peace that God imparts, and so desired to learn more of his Gospel.' He added, 'They were sure our captivity was coming to a close.'

Hermann Becker's next letter arrived, promising to bring the medicines and the 10,000 dollars. There were also welcome gifts – two tins of milk, medicine and a dollar apiece for Alfred and Arnolis.

'Tell Mr Becker to be sure and bring the money on November 16th,' they urged the departing messengers.

They began to dream of being back with their loved ones for Christmas, and prayed that they would be released before the army moved again, for Arnolis was too weak to ride a horse, still less walk.

It seemed as though their prayers would be answered. On November 18th, one of Judge Wu's men came to fetch Alfred. His manner seemed to signal that the money had arrived. He and Alfred chatted in a relaxed way as they walked towards the quarters of the hygiene squad, where Alfred was to check the medicines which Mr Becker had sent.

'You'll soon be free,' he said.

As Alfred set about his task, a doctor's wife gave him the same assurance. One of the messengers, Peter Gao, confirmed that the money had been paid. He added that Mr Becker had also sent two mountain chairs for the missionaries and was awaiting them at nearby Yongshun.

On finishing his work Alfred hurried back to share his high hopes with Arnolis. At last they were summoned by Judge Wu. For once they responded eagerly, confident of what he was about to tell them. Arnolis was still too weak to walk the distance, so Alfred carried him on his back.

'You'll be able to go back to your friends and live like aristocrats,' the guard encouraged them.

Face to face with the Judge, they had their first inkling that all was not well. His expression was hard as he handed them the articles which Mr Becker had sent for their use on the road – towel, facecloth and aniseed cake. And then the blow fell.

FREEDOM FOR ONE

'The money has come but it's only enough for one,' stated Judge Wu flatly.

Into the appalled silence, he dropped his next bombshell, 'And we've decided to release the older foreigner.'

This was the one possibility that neither Alfred nor Arnolis had envisaged. They had assumed, and been assured, that they would be released together or not at all. Why had Mr Becker ignored their urgent plea that he should pay all the money?

It soon became clear that he had not. In fact, he had sent the agreed amount – 10,000 dollars in silver: a weight of about 400 lbs which it had taken four porters to carry. But the Judge had decided that he wanted more; he had broken his word, cruelly cheating his captives.

In despairing tones Alfred said, 'Mr Becker has gone to so much trouble to get this – there is no hope of a further 10,000 dollars.'

The Judge responded with more misinformation: 'Your friends didn't send the money. It came from Chiang Kai-shek, and he'll send as much again. We have spies everywhere and it was his men who brought the money and handed it over.'

Arnolis pleaded for Alfred's release, even offering that his colleague should go in his stead, but the Judge was adamant: 'You're ill and you need attention. You must leave today. A chair is waiting. You'll be able to make several miles before dark.'

So there it was – release for Arnolis but shattered hopes for Alfred, with the prospect of yet more suffering and hardship, and all to be endured without the comfort and companionship of the person to whom he had become uniquely bonded through the extreme experiences they had shared.

Yet even at this moment Alfred heard God's silent whisper: 'I am with you always. I will never leave you nor forsake you.'

'How can I leave you with these men?' Arnolis blurted out.

'I will not be alone. God will be with me,' Alfred told him. He added, 'Tell Rose about me. Write to my parents. Remember me on Christmas Day.' Then, as the two men embraced one another, he added, 'Pray that I may recklessly preach Christ.'

Of this moment, Alfred was to write, 'I read the distress in Mr Hayman's eyes. How differently we had imagined this day. But for his family I believe he would have stayed to save me facing the winter alone.'

Alfred returned to the room he had shared with Arnolis. The guards gaped at him in unfeigned astonishment, which turned to shame with the realisation that their leaders had not proved men of their word.

'What will you do without your friend?' they asked, with concern.

'I have a friend who will never leave me,' Alfred replied. He knew his listeners understood the reference; and, even as he spoke, his own assurance deepened.

Meanwhile, after 413 days in captivity, Arnolis was free. Or so he assumed as, torn between joy and grief, he was carried along in a mountain chair to Yongshun. There he met Hermann Becker, who was delighted to see him but devastated at the empty chair which should have been carrying his colleague. For a year the negotiator had been working ceaselessly to bring about freedom for both men. Thousands had prayed, many had given generously and a number of brave volunteers had risked their lives to act as messengers. And just when it seemed as if all their efforts had succeeded, the Communists had played false.

But for the moment his urgent task was to get his sick and emaciated colleague to safety and thence to hospital as quickly as possible. They therefore pressed on to Yuanling, arriving there in a couple of days. He then hired a car to take them to Changde early the next morning.

This, it later transpired, was the last car to get away before the Communists swooped down on the district, intending to recapture Mr Hayman and seize the negotiator at the same time: a plan which would certainly have succeeded but for Hermann Becker's speedy and efficient organisation.

In Shanghai, Rhoda heard the news of her husband's release and Rose's hopes soared, assuming Alfred would soon be free too. Then the bad news was broken to her. In profound shock and disappointment, she cried out to God. What comforted her most in the days that followed were the reminders that God knew, cared and was in control, despite appearances: 'Hath God forgotten to be gracious?' 'The Lord will do great things.' 'Hope thou in God; for I shall yet praise him who is the health of my countenance.'

On December 2nd, Rhoda and Arnolis Hayman were reunited in Shanghai. As the couple entered the mission home, Rose herself generously broke the tension generated by everyone's conflicting emotions.

'Shall we sing the doxology?' she said. The familiar tune and words filled the building.

> 'How good is the God we adore,
> Our faithful, unchangeable friend,
> Whose love is as great as his power,
> And knows neither measure nor end.'

Afterwards, alone in her room, Rose wept and prayed. 'Ask and ye shall receive, that your joy may be full.' The words came into her mind before she had even opened her Bible.

'I will go on asking,' she vowed. Faith and prayer, along with the love and support of her family, friends and colleagues, were her lifelines in the long days ahead.

Deprived of human support, Alfred could only depend on God. Though he had no Bible, years of reading and studying the book and memorising verses had left him with the stored wealth of much of its teaching and stories, guidance and promises. Some of these were contained also in the one devotional book which he still had. Living up to its title, *Streams in the Desert* refreshed him again and again.

The Sunday after Arnolis had left, he read: 'Hear what the unjust judge saith. And shall not God avenge his own elect which cry day and night unto him, though he bear long with them? I tell you that he will avenge them speedily.' At once, his drooping spirits revived: God knew of his situation and would act on his behalf.

Rose, too, was a great source of inspiration. Her character, faith and love, and the hope of seeing her again, helped to still the turmoil of his emotions and drive out dark thoughts. 'When life was hardly worth cherishing,' he wrote, 'I thought of Rose and the madness went from my mind. When looking at my captors I would say, "Christ loves you and died for you," then it was easier to love them myself.'

Loving others, in Alfred's book, included telling them the truth and being straight with them. So, suspecting that the Chinese boy currently imprisoned with him had stolen a dollar from him, he tackled the lad directly: 'You'd better own up and give me my money back, and no more will be said. If not, things may go ill with you.'

The boy protested his innocence, but added, 'Perhaps your dollar fell under the bed.' A moment later, having 'searched' under the bed, he straightened up and presented Alfred with the money. That night, observing that the boy had no bedding, the missionary gave him a share of his. Early the next morning, the lad was released.

The Red Army proceeded to leave the city and take to the mountains, where the going was rough and steep. In the afternoon, Alfred was gripped by the symptoms of malaria. He took quinine and a guard kept administering smelling salts. Even so, the journey was almost unendurable.

The captain of the guard promised to find a horse for Alfred's use on the following day, and that night he invited the missionary to share his room with its glowing charcoal fire. But next day the promised ride came to very little, for the horse was so weighed down by its load of paper that it could only manage to carry Alfred a few miles. For the rest of the journey, some twenty miles, he had to manage on foot as best he could.

Next day, bombarded by the Nationalist airforce, the Red Army and its prisoners had to keep breaking ranks and running for cover.

'Aren't you frightened?' a fellow-marcher asked Alfred.

'I have an unseen friend who protects me,' said Alfred. With wry honesty, he later admitted that he was more conscious of the rheumatism in his left leg than of the bombs.

The next day the guards put the horse fully at Alfred's disposal. But by then the captain himself had also become unwell, so the two men took turns on the animal. 'In such bleak conditions' — Alfred wrote — 'captors and captives have much in common. At the frontiers of endurance men cling together. Under extreme conditions there is a common struggle for survival.'

It was Alfred's turn to walk when he heard a sudden shout from the captain who had rounded the next bend. Hurrying there with the others, Alfred saw that horse and rider had fallen off the track and into a clump of tangled bushes lower down.

They were hoisted up again, with no real harm done and everyone able to carry on as before. The outcome, Alfred reflected, might have been very different if, in his present condition, he had been the one in the saddle at the time. As if reading his thoughts one of the guards commented, 'Good thing it was the captain on the horse and not you.'

But other hazards were in store for everyone. While Alfred was on horseback they came to a stream. In riding across it he was plunged waist deep in icy water, which soaked into his bedding and left him numb and shivering.

They arrived at the city of Xupu. True to form, the army

proceeded to tear down existing posters and substitute their own, to take hostage any landlords who hadn't fled and the relatives or servants of those who had, and to confiscate their goods and chattels. The peasants were encouraged to take what they needed and urged to join the Red Army or stay and promote the Communist cause locally.

Some of the comrades showed Alfred a crucifix which had been taken from a Catholic church. 'Do you worship this?' they asked, jeeringly.

'My Saviour is alive, not on the cross,' said Alfred.

Afterwards, with genuine interest, some asked, 'Why should he have had to suffer so? Why does he wear a crown of thorns?'

'Our Lord was sinless, but the sins of the whole world were laid on him – yours and mine.'

After little more than a week, instant evacuation was ordered. Alfred only had time to snatch his haversack before leaving. He was soon to regret the things he hadn't had time to collect and bring along, particularly wool for crocheting and some magazines, spare clothes and bedding.

The pain in Alfred's legs became crippling and the guards had to half-carry him along. They were moving now not in single file but massed together. 'Criminals' and landlords taken captive in the city were securely roped and made to march as best they could along with everyone else.

Government troops were in the area. When well clear of these, the seething mass of people went into a field and were very quickly organised by the leaders into a column of orderly ranks. Discipline being re-established, the army proceeded on its way.

Each day the weather became colder and night temperatures often fell below freezing. The higher they climbed, the icier the air and the terrain. Alfred kept praying that God would give added strength to his exhausted, struggling horse; and to himself, often chilled to the bone by freezing sleet. A guard noticed his state and gave him an old but warm padded Chinese gown.

At the next town Alfred was required to write two letters – one to Rose and another to Mr Becker – asking for 10,000 dollars to be delivered without delay.

After nights in the open air people woke aching and shivering, to find that their clothes, the surrounding grasses, and even the horses' manes, had frozen stiff. In these conditions, Alfred's aches and pains grew much worse. Medication and an injection given to him by a Chinese doctor brought him some relief for a time. But life was still a battle – one which many were unable to survive.

A CHRISTMAS CARD

Another Christmas dawned, Alfred's second in captivity. He wished with all his heart that it would bring him some relief, some special flicker of hope or cheer. To be allowed even a little more rest would be a help. Even better would be permission to read Hermann Becker's latest letter, which, though brought by the courier Mr Ding some weeks earlier, he had not yet been shown.

The day was bright and sunny as they rose early and travelled through the mountains. At midday they rested. Then, despite his exhaustion, Alfred was suddenly struck by the beauty of his surroundings. Above him stretched a sky of cloudless blue; below lay the peaceful rural landscape of farm and field and rolling hills, wrapped in a dazzling blanket of snow. On a faraway hillside nestled a house which put him in mind of a Swiss chalet.

Taking all this in, Alfred was filled with wonder and excitement. His Christmas wish had been granted, for here, all around him, was a living Christmas card made by God and 'sent', on this special day, to him.

His bed that night was in a cramped shed but it resounded with Christmas carols. Alfred remembered that Jesus had been born in a stable and sang out, 'O come to my heart, Lord Jesus, there is room in my heart for thee.'

The next day, at last, and for the first time since Alfred's arrest, the marchers reached a main road. Feeling very exposed and fearing an attack from the air, the army traversed it with all possible speed. They proceeded for ten miles in safety, then travelled through some of Hunan's large market towns.

Alfred was now coming into familiar territory: a bitter-sweet experience. They passed close to a mission station – evoking memories of the busy, happy place it had once been, with its school and orphanage, hospital and chapel. Alfred wondered sadly what had happened to the missionaries and the work since the city had been captured by the Communists.

The soldiers were keen to reach Zhijiang by Chinese New Year. The news was that this city was in Communist hands, so they planned to celebrate the season by enjoying the luxuries plundered from its shops and houses.

Excitement grew as the city's pagoda became visible. With apparent lack of logic, Alfred prayed that the city would not be taken by the Communists.

The sound of firing from the city did not immediately deter the Red Army in their advance. But later, to Alfred's delight, the column changed direction and proceeded inland.

Later he learnt that there had been twenty-seven missionaries, including Mr and Mrs Becker, in the Protestant mission compound, and a number of priests and nuns in the Catholic premises.

The missionaries had been holding a service of baptism when the shooting had broken out between the Nationalist troops occupying the city and the Communist forces wanting to take it. But the ceremony had continued and everyone had been kept safe. However, Communist troops had then surrounded the city, cutting off incoming or outgoing communication and supplies. After five days of the siege, when the Nationalists had been on the point of opening the city gates, the Red Army had unexpectedly called off the siege and left.

Meanwhile, life was a continuous struggle for Alfred as the relentless marching continued. If only he could rest! He turned the thought into a prayer: 'A few days, Lord, in one place.'

The guards knew that Alfred's home was in Guizhou and questioned him about the place they were heading for, Shiqian.

But when he told them about its hot springs they were somewhat incredulous.

Soon they could see the city far below them in a gorge, its busy market street skirting the river outside the city walls. After a steep descent, they arrived there. Passing by the home of a Christian woman whom he knew, Alfred looked eagerly around but saw no one he recognised. His billet was near a chapel at which he had often preached.

Very late that night, a new prisoner joined him. The two men were soon talking like old friends. Heinrich Kellner was twenty-eight years old, a Catholic priest from Germany, educated in Rome and an accomplished linguist. He had been in China for only two years before the Communists had taken over his mission station. His colleagues had managed to get away in time, but he had been captured.

Next day, while Alfred crocheted a pair of mittens for a soldier, visitors kept coming in to stare at the new foreign captive, pass personal comments and ask interminable questions.

The priest was summoned by Judge Wu. The interrogation did not go well and he returned to his billet looking very dispirited. The Judge had set his fine at 100,000 dollars.

'I have as much right to believe in my religion as you have to believe in Communism,' he had told the Judge, only to receive the peremptory response, 'If you say another word about religion, I'll have you shot.'

The Red Army soldiers arrived fresh and rosy-faced after sampling the hot springs, but soon afterwards the army evacuated the city. As they tramped along the street, Alfred noticed a group of people looking sorrowfully towards the young priest.

'Some of our Christians,' Heinrich Kellner whispered to him. But, fearing reprisals against them, he gave no sign of recognition. Some, Alfred noticed, were in tears. The guards shouted at them to clear off and, eventually, the loyal band of supporters had to fall back and were lost to sight.

Leaving the city behind, the army crossed the river and climbed back up into the mountains. When they halted for a time, Alfred used the opportunity to continue his ongoing battle with lice – much to the astonishment and horror of the priest who had never set eyes on a body louse before. Later, noticing that Alfred had no handkerchief, he gave him one of his, apologising that it was so dirty. As far as Alfred was concerned, it was pristine.

The next day Alfred's horse was needed by a sick man and he had to struggle through driving snow on foot for many miles. He thankfully accepted the priest's offer of his mule for the final steep ascent before a halt was called.

Again they were assigned to a granary, but any hope of having an undisturbed night was dashed when a woman prisoner was brought in for questioning and then stripped and beaten.

Several hard days' travelling followed. At last, one evening Alfred had the chance to speak to Mr Yang, one of two messengers from Mr Becker who had arrived to join Mr Ding a few days earlier.

He told Alfred that the missionaries at Zhijiang were all safe and felt sure that negotiations would soon be completed for his release. Meanwhile he intended to plead with Judge Wu for a reduction of Alfred's fine.

They reached Niuchang just before Chinese New Year. Alfred and Heinrich were given a room in the home of a wealthy man. It had a very elegant Chinese bed and a charcoal brazier which threw out a welcome heat. There was also a kettle and pan for their use. Their food comprised plentiful helpings of toasted rice dough, as well as sugar cubes flavoured with maple syrup.

At last Alfred received his long-awaited summons and was soon listening to Judge Wu stipulating some new conditions. In the matter of the fine, 10,000 dollars was the least they would consider. On the other hand, if Mr Becker cooperated and supplied the things they needed, they would be prepared to pay him or reduce the fine accordingly.

First Mr Becker must apologise for suggesting that the

Communists had broken faith with him in releasing only one prisoner. Secondly, when the middlemen returned with the money they must be accompanied by General Zhang's delegate. Thirdly, two letters must be delivered to two influential men in Guangxi and their replies brought back by the delegates. Fourthly, Mr Becker must purchase a list of articles. If they cost more than the fine, the excess would be credited to Father Kellner's account.

As usual this was drafted in Chinese and Alfred was required to translate it into English for Mr Becker.

The priest was also summoned for an interview. He returned depressed after Judge Wu had outlined similarly impossible demands.

Several travelling days' later, they arrived at Dading, where they stayed in the Catholic compound. It was there that Alfred received, with great delight, a copy of his mission's report and a package from Guiyang containing, even after confiscations, socks, a sweater, bars of chocolate, a tin of milk and some coffee. Alfred and Heinrich shared these luxuries together.

Later Alfred was allowed to see and thank the messenger who had brought him the feast of good things. Joshua worked for the Guizhou missionaries and was a fine Christian man, whom Alfred already knew.

The missionaries were initially lodged in a temple and then moved into the prison. The overcrowded, insanitary conditions there reminded Alfred of Zhenjiang prison. Heinrich became seriously ill. Alfred too was unwell, with a very bad cough. The two men were occasionally visited by a doctor who also sent them some coffee. But for both of them the days seemed long and gloomy.

In these unpromising circumstances, General He Long's wife bore him a baby girl. With great joy and tenderness the general held the child in his arms. Then he sent Alfred skeins of wool, probably looted from the mission house, and asked him to make the baby some clothes. The wool came in a whole range of colours and the general also sent a pattern and a proper stainless steel crochet hook.

Alfred's stock rose considerably when the guards learnt of his new commission. With typical humour Alfred wrote later, 'With such an exalted job, it was disconcerting to keep being interrupted in order to take shelter from aircraft.'

'Can you finish by tomorrow?' Alfred was asked by a messenger one day. Assuming this indicated that they were about to break camp, Alfred plied his crochet hook late into the night, working by the light of an improvised oil lamp. At midnight the baby clothes were still unfinished, but by then he was feverish as well as exhausted from coughing.

Next morning, before dawn as they were eating breakfast, a messenger collected the unfinished garments and the unused wool.

As they travelled Alfred became increasingly ill and feverish, with a savage pain in his lower right lung and acute shortness of breath, which made it impossible for him to rest, let alone sleep. The quarrelling of other prisoners added to his sufferings. The priest was sympathetic but there was nothing he could do to help.

Unable to walk more than a few steps, Alfred was again given a horse to ride. 'Despite the guards and hostler constantly predicting an early death for the noble creature, God kept it moving,' he wrote, adding, 'I prayed a lot and ate a little.'

Judge Wu arranged for a Chinese doctor to attend Alfred. He gave him some Chinese medicine – a stew of dried orange peel, liquorice and a few other ingredients.

They entered Yunnan, keeping to the mountains where the snow had not yet melted. Heinrich Kellner was suffering badly, too ill and exhausted to eat, and too weak even to ride his mule unaided. The guards improvised a stretcher and six prisoners, slightly less weak and emaciated than the rest, took turns in carrying him on this for a few days.

A week's travelling brought them back to the border town they had occupied a week earlier. Travelling south-west, they came under daily bombardment from government aircraft and had to keep taking cover. There was little chance to rest and, often, only one meal a day, consisting mainly of corn.

March 21st was the date of Alfred's mother's birthday. Coming down from the mountains, they were at last able to enjoy something of the beauty of the Yunnan countryside in spring. Here they were surrounded by the delicate scents and pastel tints of fruit trees in blossom, and the coloured patchwork of fields growing beans, new wheat and mustard.

Alfred longed to send home a photo or picture postcard of this delightful scene. It reminded him of the verse of a hymn. He sang it softly to himself.

> 'Heaven above is softer blue,
> Earth around is sweeter green!
> Something lives in every hue
> Christless eyes have never seen.'

In Yangchang Alfred was required to translate an English Methodist newspaper found in a post office. As they moved on from there the aerial bombardment began again. On some days they had to take cover as many as twelve times, staying out of sight until the bugle sounded the 'all clear'. The physical exertion, particularly the constant mounting and dismounting of his horse, exacerbated Alfred's painful leg condition.

'How are you?' General Xiao Ke asked him one day. A little surprised by the question but taking it at face value, he responded, 'My cough's somewhat better, but my limbs are weak.'

He was totally unprepared for the General's next words.

'We have decided to differentiate between foreigners in future,' Xiao Ke began. 'You're a Swiss citizen and Switzerland is not an imperialistic country. You have no unequal treaties with China, neither have you any concessions, so we have decided to free you tomorrow.'

Alfred had longed and prayed to hear just such words – but did he dare believe them? Torn between hope and caution, he heard the

General continue, 'We will not release the priest. He's from Hitler's country – no friend of Communists.'

As the General left, the priest, who had been close enough to hear what had been said, came across and magnanimously offered his congratulations. As he shook Heinrich's hand, Alfred was torn between hope and joy for himself and sadness and sympathy for his friend, just as Arnolis had been in a similar situation six months earlier. Moreover, as he told the priest, the Communists had broken faith with him before, so he wouldn't be doing any celebrating until he was actually free.

In the meantime the army continued to traverse, perilously, Yunnan's hills and valleys. On the heights the fierce winds for which the province was famous threatened to sweep the marchers off their feet. In the valleys they whipped up dust-storms, and the comrades had to tie handkerchiefs over their faces to keep the choking particles from getting into their mouths and noses.

RELEASE

Alfred was resting at the next village when a messenger approached to say, 'General Xiao invites you and the priest to dine with him this evening.' Noticing the state of the prisoners' dress, he added that some smartening up might not come amiss.

'We have no other garments,' said Alfred.

'Communists don't stand on ceremony,' the messenger replied, sidestepping neatly and getting in the last word at the same time.

There were ten guests in all, including General Zhang and a man named Wang Zhen, a Sixth Army political commissar. As they ate, General Xiao began a conversation with Heinrich Kellner on the subject of German military tactics. Then he broke off to observe pointedly to Alfred, 'Switzerland has no standing army, so of course you had no military training.' The significance of this differentiation between the two nations and their 'representatives' became clear when, towards the end of the meal, the General said, addressing himself solely to Alfred, 'We intend to release you tomorrow.'

In a private aside, Mr Wang suggested that the word 'tomorrow' should not necessarily be taken literally. The thought had already occurred to Alfred but he thanked the official for the tip.

After the meal the guards escorted the missionaries back to their quarters with due deference, as befitted those who had been guests of a Red Army general. But soon it was business as usual, as the orders came to break camp and the prisoners were hustled along as the comrades tried to stay one jump ahead of the Nationalist infantry in the rear without coming under fire from its airforce.

It was April before they reached Tawan. There, they travelled along narrow muddy paths between terraces of waterlogged rice-fields. People and animals were constantly losing their footing. Once Alfred was flung off his horse into the mud. Afterwards he would have felt safer walking, but as this would have entailed breaking rank, his request to go under his own steam was turned down.

Later, Alfred was approached by a soldier bringing a message from the Judge. 'We are going to release you. Judge Wu wants to speak to you,' he said, and then escorted Alfred into the city. Judge Wu and his wife arrived in time to watch the missionary dismounting very gingerly from his horse – a sight which seemed to afford them some amusement, although afterwards the Judge gave instructions that the prisoner should be taken to his billet to rest until he was sent for.

The guard duly escorted him to a loft in a nearby house, where Heinrich Kellner was already resting. After eating a late midday meal, Alfred lay down too, though not for long. When the summons came he got up and began to gather up his things, until the guard stopped him with the words, 'You needn't bring anything with you.'

The Judge seemed to be in a good mood. He had a new lamp which he wanted Alfred to help him get working. After translating the instructions into Chinese, Alfred was able to tell the judge that he'd been using the wrong oil. To his surprise, the Judge then invited him to a feast. Other guests included General Xiao Ke, General Zhang and the political commissar.

'When you report to the newspapers, you must remember we are friends,' Wang Zhen instructed Alfred. 'You have seen how good we are to the poor, how we work on principle and are not common bandits as we are slanderously reported to be.' The Judge added, 'We shall be glad to hear from you if you care to correspond.'

'I've no objection to you remaining in China as a visitor,' General

Xiao Ke chipped in, 'and should even permit you to have a school if you would only refrain from drugging the scholars and populace with this belief in God. But I think it would be better if you went home and stayed there.'

After the General had left, Alfred turned to the Judge and spoke up on behalf of the priest. 'If you want him to live until the fine weather comes, you will have to see that he receives better care,' he warned him, adding, 'Could you not give him an orderly as you have General Zhang? Someone to get him water for drinking or washing, and make sure he has fuel and enough straw for a bed?'

'Impracticable,' was the Judge's response, but he promised to see that the priest got proper medical attention. Then he said, 'You will be taken to the house of a commoner where you must stay till dawn. We move shortly after midnight but you mustn't start before dawn. Then you'll be free to go.'

He pointed out that Alfred had been guilty of preaching the gospel, and so his release was conditional on his not transgressing in that way again. Finally, he gave the missionary ten silver dollars for food and told him that he would be able to reach the capital in two days.

The priest was asleep when he returned to the loft. Alfred woke him to say goodbye, hand him half the money he'd just received and promise to do all he could to secure his release. Then: 'We kissed each other and mutually confessed and forgave each other's shortcomings.'

Decades later, Alfred learnt the sad news that ten days after his release, Heinrich Kellner had died. His body had been placed in a beautiful coffin confiscated from a wealthy man and taken off for burial. But the men paid to do the task had merely left the coffin on a hillside and absconded: a sad ending to the earthly life of a young, well-motivated and gifted man.

Having parted from his companion, Alfred was escorted to another house where he lay down and rested, to be roused by bugle calls and the stir and bustle of vast numbers of people getting up and preparing to leave. There followed the steady, seemingly unending tramp of marching feet as the Red Army moved on – minus one very excited prisoner and his party. Finally, at dawn, all was quiet.

Then came the sound of a door being opened. Two young grooms, terrified deserters from the Red Army, had crept into the house. They begged to be allowed to go to Kunming with the group. Given permission, they set off with the leaving party, going on ahead, while Alfred hobbled painfully along behind, accompanied by the faithful Joshua, the messenger from Guizhou.

Alfred was free at last – after 2,500 miles and 560 days in captivity. Free to savour the present moment, in the pleasant, peaceful surroundings of a stream and wooded hills, bathed in spring sunshine, and to begin to anticipate all kinds of future joys.

Joshua spoke of his difficulties in getting through the Communist lines but was modest and self-deprecating when Alfred attempted to thank him for all he had done. In fact, seeing Alfred's difficulties in walking, he reproached himself for not having done enough.

'Stay here and I will arrange a chair for you,' he told the missionary.

'Before you go, Joshua, do you know what day it is?' Alfred asked.

'No,' Joshua replied, adding, 'Is it Sunday?'

'Yes, but a very special Sunday,' Alfred replied. 'It's Easter Sunday. Don't you think it's wonderful that these men who've so often taunted me that Jesus is dead, that he could not help me, that these men who said I would not be free until the last cent was paid, should have unwittingly set me free on Easter morning?'

It was an unforgettable moment of shared joy. Afterwards Joshua went to make arrangements at a nearby farmhouse, leaving Alfred to continue to wonder not just at the timing of his release, but at the very fact of it, given that no further money or supplies had arrived from the mission since Arnolis had been set free six months earlier. To revel more deeply in the peace and quiet of his surroundings, after eighteen months of constant surveillance by over 300 different guards, and the noise and bustle of hordes of people. To relish, above all, the prospect of being reunited with Rose, and then with other friends and loved ones. To dream of home, of rest and stability, after being billeted in hundreds of different attics, granaries or bleak rooms of one sort or another, amid all the rigours and uncertainties of being held captive by the Red Army and having no option but to keep up with its tortuous and harried progress through the mountains and plains of south-west China.

Before long, Joshua returned with news that a litter had been found. But first he carried Alfred to the farmhouse where they ate breakfast. Then he settled the missionary in the mountain chair, and accompanied the porters bearing it along. 'As I was little more than skin and bones,' Alfred commented wryly, 'the men were not over-taxed.'

At the city there was an hour's tantalising delay, as government troops questioned the new arrivals and searched their belongings. Then, guarded by soldiers holding fixed bayonets, they were taken to see the Nationalist general. Alfred's beard seemed to have triggered off the suspicion that he was a Russian spy.

The general and his officers were in a temple eating their evening meal. Seeing Alfred, he rose and came towards him with the words, 'Oh, you're the Swedish gentleman who has been held captive for so long.'

'Swiss,' Alfred corrected him, politely.

The general nodded. 'I'll see you are taken safely to the capital tomorrow but we must find a place for you to sleep tonight.' This proved to be the Pentecostal Mission. The woman in charge was under great pressure, with soldiers occupying every spare inch of the place. But she found the travellers a bundle of straw and took them to the room normally used for storing firewood. In the morning, after breakfast, Alfred was given a chair and a bodyguard and soon the little party set off for their thirty-mile journey.

Alfred thought that no one would yet know that he had been set free. But he was wrong. About four miles from the city, he saw three foreigners approaching on horseback. After a while they dismounted and waited. On reaching them, Alfred alighted from his chair to meet them. Only then did he realise that they were fellow-missionaries, George Metcalf, Gladstone Porteous and Albert Allen, the advance guard of his welcome party.

Alfred was offered one of their horses and helped into the saddle. As he rode along, he asked the others how they had known of his release.

'The military in the capital received a telephone message saying that you would be coming escorted by soldiers,' they replied. A larger welcome party was waiting for them a little further on. They broke into the doxology as Alfred approached.

It was an emotional moment for everyone. Alfred recorded his personal, and very typical, response later: 'My heart leapt for joy, lifting me out of my weariness, as I remembered God's presence. I had come from the shadows but the light had accompanied me. A longing to give my freedom back to him possessed me.'

Within a week from Alfred's release, Rose was by her husband's bedside. The 2,000 mile journey from Shanghai to Kunming would have taken a fortnight by boat and train, but Rose went by plane – her first ever flight – and covered the distance in a day and a half.

'Our joy was full, our cup running over,' wrote Alfred. And Rose: 'The year and a half of separation seemed to belong to another world and it was as if we had never parted. No words can describe our joy and heartfelt praise to God as we met again.'

While they rejoiced and Alfred began to recover, the Sixth and Second Armies marched on. They were to arrive in Shaanxi in October to join the troops which had been there since the previous September or October. The cost of all the journeyings comprising the Long March, in terms of lives, was to prove colossal. Estimates suggest that of the 100,000 marchers who set out with the main army, only about a tenth remained after the 6,000 mile journey.

The rest had died or dropped out, having failed or given up the attempt to survive the battle against the elements, the terrain, the conditions and their human enemies. For those left to hold the fort in Jiangxi, resisting and harrying an enemy vastly outnumbering and far better equipped than them, life had proved equally grim with comparable losses.

Famously surviving those perilous times, indeed emerging from them very much in control of the Party and the Red Army, was Mao Zedong. When the March had started, he had been overshadowed by Communist leaders favouring the Russian revolutionary line. But after the Battle of the Xiang River, in which the Red Army had sustained huge losses, things had begun to change.

In January 1935 – when the two missionary captives had been 'paying' for their pre-Christmas escape attempt – Mao had been readmitted to the inner circle of Communist leadership. This historic event had taken place at Zunyi, Alfred's first mission station, and afterwards, implementing his ideas and plans, Mao had led his column of marchers north-eastwards to arrive at Shaanxi in October, a month before Arnolis' release.

Since then, while Alfred had continued to footslog through Guizhou and Hunan, he had been consolidating his leadership and supervising the recovery, reconstruction and expansion of the People's Republic – another face of Communism that Alfred and Rose were to encounter – but not before some fifteen eventful busy years had passed.

Rose's and the doctors' first priority was to get Alfred well again. On his release, his physical condition had been very poor indeed. Skin and bone, he was also found to be suffering from pleurisy, bronchitis, beri-beri and sprue. One doctor said he would not have survived another ten days had he not been set free. He added that what the missionary had been through would shorten his life by ten years – a prediction which was to cause Alfred much gentle amusement later on.

After seven weeks' rest, he was back to his normal weight and free of pleurisy and bronchitis. After four more, the doctor allowed him to get up and walk round the room.

From his sick bed in Kunming, he dictated an account of his captivity which was published as *The Restraining Hand* by Hodder and Stoughton. Within two or three months, the book had gone into a second edition.

Eventually, in late summer, he was deemed fit to travel back to Europe. But he was still far from robust, needing medication, care and rest. Such considerations, however, did not prevent him from living life to the full. Indeed, the next four years were strenuous by anyone's standards.

During that time he and Rose travelled extensively, visiting and fulfilling speaking engagements in Britain, Switzerland, Belgium, Canada and America. Among the highlights for Alfred was the chance to speak in Winterthur, the town which his father had left fifty-eight years earlier; and to visit Oberuzwil, his mother's native village.

Together they experienced moving reunions and celebrations with family and friends, including a meeting in Three Hills, Alberta, Canada with Charlie, Alfred's cousin and adopted brother who had emigrated thirty-five years earlier.

And, at packed gatherings in many countries, they both shared their experiences, emphasising not their own courage or endurance but God's faithfulness, and urging their listeners to trust and obey him wholeheartedly. Elizabeth Archibald remembers the vast numbers of people who crowded into the Albert Hall Manchester for one such meeting, and how moved everyone felt at hearing what the couple had to say. In particular, she recalls Rose's contribution.

'In her charmingly simple way she told of the long waiting days in Shanghai, and of a child who came and asked her one day, "Mrs Bosshardt, are you sometimes lonely?" "Yes, I am," Rose replied. "Then, when you are lonely, you can come and play with me," the child told her.

'She also spoke of how another child in England prayed for

Alfred's release every time she said grace before meals: "Thank you for breakfast (dinner, tea), and please give Uncle Bosshardt something to eat and set him free soon." Her parents were astonished that this eight-year-old never once forgot to mention Alfred during his captivity until Easter Day when he was released. That day, she omitted praying for him. Curious, the mother asked her daughter, "Have you forgotten someone?" The child looked thoughtful, then responded confidently, "O, you mean Uncle Bosshardt. I don't need to pray for him any more – he's all right." And at the time that she spoke those words in England, the news of Alfred's release on Easter Day had not yet reached even his wife and friends in China.'

Public meetings gave Rose and Alfred opportunities to share such moving stories, and to thank the thousands of people of all ages who had worked, prayed and sent money for their release. They and the mission paid particular tribute to the courage and persistence of Hermann Becker and the Chinese messengers during the months of negotiations.

They returned to China via America. This being 1939, after the outbreak of the Second World War, their journey across the Atlantic was perilous. But they arrived safely in New York, and then visited Paterson, New Jersey, to stay with the Stam family, whose son and daughter-in-law had been executed five years earlier.

Why should Alfred and Arnolis have been released, and John and Betty murdered? It was a question that exercised Alfred and Rose, like many others. But the Stam family spoke rather of 'the infinite wisdom and goodness of God, of his divine will; and of the 700 students who had stood up in the Memorial Service held in Moody Bible Institute, to consecrate their lives to missionary work wherever God called them'.

Alfred wrote:

'We left the Stams cherishing a new experience of God. It was said that the tragedy opened deep springs of faith and love in countless hearts.

They still flow today. As their story is retold, the vision continues to dawn on young people of the privilege of sacrifice and suffering in fellowship with Christ. We were called to live for Christ, they to die for him.'

Extraordinary experiences can throw the rest of life into permanent anticlimax for one reason or another. Those involved can be pushed beyond breaking point and never fully recover. Or, taking the easy way out and succumbing to pride and unreality, they can subsequently devote themselves to replaying and basking in 'their finest hour' ever afterwards. The Long March did not have this effect on the lives of Alfred and Rose. The strain and suffering involved, and the media attention, publicity and other pressures afterwards, could easily have broken or spoilt them in those or other ways. Instead, they were able to move on from their extraordinary fiery ordeal into the next stage of their lives, having matured and deepened in character and faith through it.

They would have attributed this to the presence of God and the prayers, love and support of family and friends. But contributory factors must have included the straightforward way they saw life, as coming from God's hands, and their trust in him, spilling over into their receptive, open attitudes towards others.

Mr Chai, Mr Yang and Mr He (left to right) — the three Chinese messengers who acted as go-betweens for Hermann Becker.

Rhoda and Arnolis Hayman with Theo, Joy, David, Andrew, Frances and Ben, probably a year or two after Arnolis's release in 1935.

The Bosshardts in Kunming, Yunnan, two months after Alfred's release in 1936. Alfred had got out of bed to put on the new suit Rose had brought for him from Shanghai to celebrate their fifth wedding anniversary. This was the first time she had seen him in western clothes!

Alfred Bosshardt in 1936 in or near Kunming after his release. He travelled in a mountain chair, then one of the missionaries in his welcome party offered him a horse.

Arnolis Hayman in 1935 soon after his release from captivity after 413 days with the Red Army.

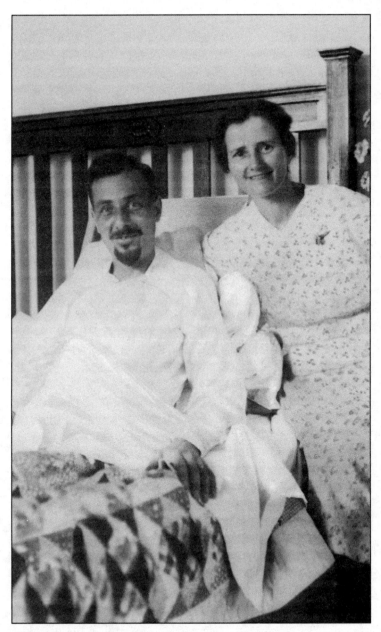

Alfred and Rose united in a hospital in Kunming, Yunnan, Easter 1936, after eighteen months separation.

CHINA – 1940-1951

THE RETURN

Christmas Day 1940. Alfred and Arnolis are in church in Shanghai together. Arnolis looks at Alfred and says one word: 'Emmanuel.' Instantly, both men are transported back six years to their Christmas in captivity together, when the reminder that God was with them brought joy flooding back into their hearts and faces.

Rose and Alfred plan to return to inland China, to the very province in which they were taken captive. This is not an act of bravado, still less an exercise in nostalgia. It is simply a matter of continuing obedience.

But while waiting to travel to Guizhou, they have the joy of staying with the Haymans in their apartment at the mission premises at Shanghai. Alfred and Arnolis spend time visiting the prison, and he and Rose accept a temporary appointment to oversee the men's hostel at the Bible Seminary.

Shanghai prison is well managed and clean but conditions are spartan in the extreme. Prisoners have two blankets and one container for rubbish.

There are thirty men in the condemned cells – all awaiting execution. The missionaries visit each of them with the message of God's love and forgiveness. Alfred senses that one of these, an eighteen-year-old found guilty of murder, seems to be hanging on his every word. He feels sure that the lad is able to grasp the essentials of the Christian message.

Another prisoner tells him, 'The Saviour is only for those who have money. They can go to heaven.' Alfred assures him that money is irrelevant where salvation is concerned, illustrating the point with Jesus' story of the rich man and Lazarus. On his next visit, the prisoner is eager to hear and learn more.

On that same Christmas Day, Alfred and Rose received their finest Christmas present: the news that they would be joining a party leaving for inland China in January.

To their added joy, they learnt that they were to go to Tongzhou mission station to work with Louisa Köhler. It seemed an ideal appointment. Apart from the fact that they loved and admired their Swiss colleague, living and working at Tongzhou would fulfil the conditions that the doctor deemed necessary for Alfred at that time: access to medical facilities, nourishing food, and not too much responsibility.

But suddenly all that changed. The Bosshardts were asked to take charge of a newly opened station in Panxian. With only four baptised Christians and no missionaries there, it was hardly what the doctor had ordered. Rose and Alfred agreed to the posting, but struggled with feelings of acute disappointment for some time.

The journey to Guizhou provided some unwanted drama, when a snapped steering column sent their bus out of control, to end up in a gully on its side. The passengers, considerably shaken up but thankful to be alive, effected their escape by crawling out of a window.

Arriving safe and sound in their 'home' province, Rose and Alfred felt their spirits rise as their eyes took in the familiar countryside. Hillsides where azaleas and wild roses spread bright skeins of colour brought back a host of memories.

A member of the British Embassy offered them a lift in his car, and they travelled speedily and comfortably along through Qingzhen, where they had honeymooned, and on to Guiyang. From there they travelled to Tongzhou for a brief compensatory stay with their friend and colleague, Louisa Köhler.

The mission station lay in an excavated hillside. With her own money – including specially designated gifts – the missionary had bought the land and paid for the building work. The premises, built to Louisa's design and specifications and using local stone, comprised her home and magnificent garden, a chapel, an outhouse, a dispensary and bookroom.

This remarkable woman was now aged sixty-one and working alone. The Chinese called her 'grandmother' and 'venerable teacher', and her medical skill had saved many people's lives.

Standing by the Christian cemetery, she told Rose and Alfred, 'I have more of my people in heaven than on earth.' Local Christians who had met violent deaths were buried there, including her adopted son, murdered because he had spoken out against some evil practice.

Rose was in tears when it came time to say goodbye. Louisa had truly cherished her guests, sharing her home and herself with them, and sending them off with beautifully made cloth shoes and other presents. Alfred was to write: 'In life we can sometimes accept the big trials more easily than the small disappointments. We had been able to take my captivity as being in the purposes of God. It was harder to accept that we could not remain with Miss Köhler.'

But in Panxian there was work for the Bosshardts to do, and a house and Chinese cook waiting for them. On their first Sunday, fifty people came to the service in the guest hall. It was good to be back with the Chinese people, and Alfred and Rose quickly opened their home and their hearts to them.

Like all CIM missionaries, they had been charged to facilitate the development of an independent, locally-run Chinese church from which they could and should, at the right time, withdraw. No easy task, this, with only four full church members – none of whom, as Alfred humorously commented, would have struck a job consultant as ideal candidates. Appearances, however, can be deceptive.

There was Mrs Ge Lai, elderly, blind and illiterate, who – against all the odds – was to become a very effective Christian worker. And Huan San-niang, the Bosshardts' cook, aged forty. She had worked hard at reading Chinese and was now able to follow the Bible passages as they were read out. Also Mr Fu, aged forty-five who had two years' education and could read relatively fluently. And finally, Mr Gao, who had received more schooling than the others. These were the nucleus, but other less committed people also attended services.

Having managed for a year without a missionary, the congregation felt ready to sit back. But Alfred and Rose had no intention of 'doing it all'. Among other things, they started a monthly church business meeting to encourage everyone's involvement and initiative.

There was often a price to pay for those who showed any degree of interest or commitment towards Christianity in a predominantly Buddhist society. Some wives who attended meetings were beaten by their husbands and an old woman was turned out of her home by other members of her family.

The Bosshardts ran twelve meetings a week, including family prayers, as well as visiting people in their homes. Alfred made contact with the chief magistrate. He was not a Christian, he said, but had read much of the Old and New Testaments. Alfred asked him for permission to visit the local prison. Very politely, his request was refused. The missionary accepted this, biding his time.

He and Rose were beginning to feel at home in this city between the mountains. They grew flowers and vegetables in their garden and kept a ready welcome in their home for all visitors.

Attendances rose. The guest hall was becoming over-full. It was time to pray for a chapel of their own. Each Sunday, for half an hour, some of the Christians gathered to ask God to meet this need. Their funds were small but their faith large.

And very soon they had their chapel. A businessman insisted that they should use the middle floor of his three-storey building. The rent was to be minimal. Up until then, the army had been billeting soldiers there. Now the owner put up a notice stating that the place was for church use.

While church members were cleaning the premises, some

soldiers suddenly arrived. In an atmosphere that had suddenly become electric, Alfred quietly explained the change of use, then politely requested that the army should find other quarters. The soldiers accepted this without a fuss, and everyone breathed a sigh of relief at the sound of their boots clattering down the stairs.

Gradually the building was furnished and fitted out. Pews, paid for by local Christians, replaced the existing seats. A beautiful new communion table was made and given as a memorial for the church's first pastor, Mr Crapuchettes, killed in a road accident. On its black lacquered top – a speciality of the area – were carved in Chinese characters some words of Jesus: 'Do this in remembrance of me.'

The chapel was decorated for their first Christmas there. Three women were baptised in the river that day and afterwards those present ate a festive meal of sunflower seeds, rice cakes and melon slices, and sang carols.

One effect of the war, ongoing during their first four years in Panxian, was to cause disruption and delay in the postal services between Europe and Asia. A letter home could take up to nine months to arrive. Also, there were shortages in the supply of food, clothes and household goods, with resulting price rises. But the missionaries found that their needs were always met.

One day Alfred's patience in one respect was at last rewarded: the magistrate gave him permission to visit the men's prison and Rose, the women's. The inequalities of the system were quickly apparent to them. Those with money and families were given private rooms, where relatives could visit them, bringing food and clothing. The rest were poor, malnourished and, often, sick. Some made straw sandals to sell, or lived on the wealthy prisoners' left-overs.

Alfred noticed that rice water was being thrown away and arranged for it to be kept and given to the poorer prisoners. This at least contained a certain amount of nourishment.

Some American soldiers were billeted in the area. When Alfred called to see them, an orderly was about to throw away some burnt glutinous rice.

'Could I have that for the prisoners?' he asked. The young American officer to whom he'd addressed this question couldn't believe that anyone would be desperate enough to eat such stuff. Alfred took him to the prison to see for himself. As the burnt rice was produced, the prisoners started pushing their bowls through the bars, desperate to be noticed and served before supplies ran out. The watching officer could barely restrain his tears.

The work continued quietly, with occasional conferences and holidays. The Bosshardts moved house and their colleague and former fellow-captive Grace Emblen came on a six-week visit. Then Rose fell ill, and was feverish with a high temperature for five days. Alfred sponged her down with alcohol. Her temperature suddenly dropped, and for nine days she seemed to be getting better. Then it soared and she lay in bed, groaning, her breathing growing fainter.

Alfred was at her bedside, along with Louisa Köhler, who was visiting, a Chinese Christian colleague, Mrs Dan, and a Chinese doctor. Together, long and earnestly, they prayed.

Within two hours Rose's temperature had returned to normal. After that, she slowly recovered.

The year the war ended, there was the joy of a baptism. Samuel Tang's father, a lapsed Christian and an opium addict, had nevertheless taught his three daughters and one son about Jesus, and Samuel had been brought along when the Bosshardts had come to the mission station.

At first the boy had shown little interest in the Christian message. Then his father had died and Samuel had had to grow up fast and assume his responsibilities as head of the household. It was then that he had sustained severe burns through a domestic fire. These had been treated by Mrs Dan, who had also spoken to him about Christ and found him changed and very receptive.

After becoming a Christian, Samuel matured well. Alfred saw

him as someone with leadership potential, and Samuel himself felt that God was calling him to study and train for responsibility in the church.

Alfred and Rose visited Switzerland for the 90th birthday celebrations of Maman Piaget. At the special service ninety-six family members were present, and Alfred played the organ voluntary, 'He shall feed his flock.' This was followed by a lunch and later on a picnic tea.

The next year, 1948, after falling and breaking her hip, just before her 91st birthday, Rose's mother died. Alfred's father died in the same year and his mother began to show signs of frailty.

In Panxian, the church helped Samuel to become a student at the Chongqing Theological Seminary. The Communists took over Chongqing before he was through his studies, but he managed to graduate and return to Panxian. At a church meeting there he was elected pastor. Completely loyal to Christ and at the same time prepared to work with the authorities whenever possible, he set about getting the church registered – a long and difficult procedure.

The mission sent a letter to all their staff saying that those who wished to leave the country were free to do so. Alfred and Rose prayed and decided that they would stay until the mission was forced to withdraw completely.

THE TAKE-OVER

After sixteen years Alfred found himself once again living under the Communist regime. During those years the threat to China from Japan had intensified and Chiang Kai-shek had been forced to form an anti-Japanese alliance with the Communists. But after America entered the war in 1941 he had left it largely to American forces to defeat Japan, while he deployed his in a renewed attack on the Communists.

Hostilities continued until 1949 when Chiang was defeated and fled to Taiwan and Mao Zedong proclaimed the People's Republic of China and masterminded the systematic take-over of the whole country by the Communists.

As in many other places, Panxian fell to the Party without a shot. Alfred must have had a strong sense of *déjà vu* as the Red soldiers entered the city, singing a violent anti-Chiang Kai-shek song, and then proceeded to put up their propaganda posters.

Predictably the landlords were the first to feel the brunt of the new regime. The man who had given the church its premises was one of these: he was ordered to donate a huge quantity of rice. Otherwise, for a time, life continued relatively undisturbed.

Then came restrictions, one after another. First the Christians were forbidden to propagate their faith outside the chapel – putting paid to open-air services and home visits.

Secondly the mission schools were closed. The headmasters of both the Protestant and Catholic primary schools were summoned to the local magistrates' courts and accused of running inefficient establishments. Their protests fell on deaf ears. But as Alfred wrote, 'Later, we saw God's overruling. If the schools had remained open, eventually we would have been compelled to use Communist primers and Communist teachers.'

Beggars were given new clothes and recruited as spies. When they had done their work of reporting on everyone, they were cast off as worthless non-producers. The climate of fear and distrust escalated as people were encouraged or pressurised into making accusations against others. No one knew who was going to be imprisoned next. Suicide became a way out for many.

Everyone had to attend indoctrination classes and Christians were asked to recant. Only one of the seventy church members did so – under great pressure from her son, a Red Army soldier. And when people had to state their religious or political affiliations, 200 families registered themselves as Christians.

Alfred conducted three baptisms at different times. At the third, there were eleven candidates. Afterwards, on the way back from the riverside, the two Chinese leaders who had taken part were arrested. Alfred, protesting on their behalf, was kicked and then taken away, at gun point, for questioning. The type of questioning must have been ominously familiar to him.

Why was he in China and what was he doing? His background and motives were scrutinised, and his replies recorded. Recent events were probed in the same way. Was it wise to immerse candidates on a winter's day? Alfred replied that seventy people had been baptised since he'd arrived in Panxian without suffering any ill effects from the experience. He was given a stern talking to and then released, as were his Chinese colleagues.

Alfred faced a second Christmas in Panxian under the Communists. Though not a prisoner as he had been during his two earlier Christmasses under the regime, he was nevertheless subject to considerable restraints. He and the Catholic priest were not to leave town, and their passports were confiscated by the chief magistrate. Again traditional Chinese courtesy went by the board, and the missionaries were made to feel that they were *persona non grata*.

Canadian colleagues Anna and Alban Douglas were expecting their first child. While waiting for a pass to go to the mission hospital at Anshun, Anna was suddenly taken very ill. Even then the authorities refused to grant a travel permit to a nurse who would have come to help. The baby was stillborn but thanks to Rose's midwifery skills and to prayer, the mother survived.

Alfred's mother died in 1951, a year that was to be memorable both in the history of the mission and of Communism in China. While the Party launched campaigns against counter-revolutionaries, corruption, waste and bureaucracy, the mission advised its members to leave. Their continuing presence, it was suggested, might be making things harder rather than easier for local Christians. Taking the advice of their members, Rose and Alfred applied for permission to travel.

Accusations, trials and executions increased. Immense pressure was put on particular tenants to denounce their landlord – who was also the proprietor of the house in which Rose and Alfred lived. But it came to nothing: the man had always been very fair in his dealings, so no evidence could be produced against him.

The officials did not let the matter rest there. One night the police entered the man's home and accused him of falsifying papers. He denied this, but was arrested. When the authorities had taken what they wanted of his possessions, they opened his home up to be ransacked by all comers. His wife was devastated: she had been virtually widowed and pauperised overnight, without hope of help or redress.

Another woman, Mrs Liu, was deprived of her teaching job when the primary school was closed down. Her husband had been planning to open a medicine shop before he'd become ill and died. To support herself and their child, she sold some of his clothing and then began making socks and scarves to sell.

The Communists objected: she must be categorised and operate either as a business woman or as a manual worker; she couldn't have it both ways.

Her house was frequently searched. She told the officials, truthfully, that the medicines she had were those which her husband had bought and intended to sell. Not long afterwards they told her that someone – unnamed – had accused her or her husband of stealing the medicines.

She went to ask Alfred for advice. 'Tell the truth, don't lie,' he urged her. In all, the officials came eight times, pressing her for an admission of guilt. When she wouldn't give them one, they sent two women to persuade her to say that her husband had stolen the goods. Such a confession, they said, wouldn't hurt him and would ensure that she wasn't sent to prison. The latter consideration, they suggested, should surely weigh heavily with her, if only for the sake of her elderly mother and young son.

Resisting this emotional pressure, she refused to comply with the women's wishes. They became very angry. Later an armed officer arrived to thrust a piece of paper at her, telling her that it contained a declaration of her husband's guilt, and ordering her to sign it. She shot up a desperate prayer for guidance, then asked when her husband was alleged to have stolen the medicines. The man named a date.

'That was two and a half years ago,' Mrs Liu said. The man agreed.

'My husband died three and a half years ago,' Mrs Liu told him, adding, 'and I'll take you to his grave where the date is carved in stone.' Thus silenced, the official left.

Later, Mrs Liu's elderly mother expressed her wish to return to the place where she had been born and raised. Since she was too infirm to walk, she needed authorisation to travel by sedan chair. Remarkably, she received it, along with the offer of four porters to carry the chair. The services of these men were paid for from the sale of the medicines – a happy outcome only made possible because Mrs Liu, refusing to lie, had eventually been vindicated.

The months went by and still the missionaries waited for the return of their passports and for permission to leave. Meanwhile they tried to sell their possessions to raise some money for their expenses and donate a percentage to the refugees.

This did not go down well. They were told they must either give their things away or leave them behind. Samuel Tang advised the Bosshardts to write a letter listing the items they would be giving to the authorities. Alfred did this, ending his letter with a reminder that he and Rose had been awaiting their pass for some months.

Reading this, the magistrate's face registered delight until he reached the last sentence. Then he threw the paper down, shouting, 'What's this? Are you trying to buy your pass?'

He ordered Alfred to rewrite the letter, listing as before what he would be giving to the Communists but adding the phrase, 'with a willing heart'. Five copies of this amended letter were required. Weeks went by and still no pass had arrived for Alfred and Rose, while other missionaries elsewhere were on the move.

At last Alfred was summoned. To his surprise he was told that he would be given a letter authorising the magistrate in Guiyang to release the passes which he and Rose needed. Normally missionaries were required to advertise their intention to leave through a newspaper, repeated the procedure twice, and then waiting for possible objections to be raised. But the official insisted, 'All you want is a letter from me. We had a meeting to discuss you. Everyone said you were good people and so we are all your guarantors.'

Alfred was to see God's hand in this departure from normal procedure. Had they advertised, someone reading the paper might have responded by accusing the missionaries of continuing to preach the gospel. Such an infringement of the conditions imposed on them could have led to their being refused permission to leave.

A friend of the magistrate called to say, 'If you really want to go, leave your pressure cooker and meat-grinder. The magistrate is coming again and when he sees these things put aside you will have your pass. This must be kept a secret.'

The magistrate duly returned with the letter authorising the missionaries' passes. Alfred invited the man to inspect what they were taking. He lifted the lid of a box, then said, 'These are your personal effects, you will have absolutely no trouble.'

The next morning six prisoners arrived to collect all that had been 'donated' to the Communists. Then the truck in which they were to travel arrived, and at last they were on their way. They reached Hong Kong safely, their luggage having been inspected eight times *en route*.

After nearly three decades in the country, Alfred and Rose were now out of China. Along with all the other missionaries similarly expelled they wondered what would happen to the Christians left behind to cope with a regime that denied the very existence of God; and whether they would ever see or even hear of any of them again.

Leaving China was an appalling wrench for countless missionaries who loved the country and people and had been engaged in evangelism, medical or educational work, sometimes all three, for many years. The experience was akin to bereavement with all the attendant feelings of shock, loss, disorientation, anger, fear and pain.

They all lost their country of adoption and their work there. Those in the China Inland Mission also lost the name of their fellowship. And where deep loyalties and long commitment are involved, the short answer to the question, 'What's in a name?' is 'Plenty!'

Some missionaries stayed with the mission to continue their work elsewhere. Whatever changes and adjustments were entailed for these people, they still had the security of belonging to the mission and being able to draw on its resources, including its fellowship, and news and prayer networks.

Others, for whatever reason, left the mission to find new work, roles and identities. The changes and adjustments for them were far greater – and all of them had to be faced without the familiar and reassuring framework and benefits of mission membership. It was hardly surprising that many in this situation felt very bereft and vulnerable indeed.

Alfred and Rose did not experience this degree of upheaval and pain, for they chose, when invited to do so, to remain as missionaries, albeit in a new environment. Their expulsion from China had not, they believed, rescinded their call from God to take the Christian message to the Chinese people.

Nor, as time would tell, had it destroyed the work already done. In 1991, forty years after the Bosshardts had left Panxian, Alfred received a letter from Minnie Kent, who had been a lecturer at Chongqing Theological Seminary and also involved with the Panxian church.

It said:

'I have had a letter from Samuel Tang ... We left Panxian church in his charge and have not heard any word from him since 1951 until yesterday. He is still pastor of the church, also vice-chairman of a group of churches in five adjacent counties for which we were responsible. When we left there was a well organised church of seventy baptised members. Samuel reports that now there are a hundred churches in this large area and 10,000 believers. More than we asked or thought!'

LAOS – 1951-1966

THE NEXT CITY

'When they persecute you in one city, flee to the next.' Reading these words, Alfred and Rose considered what places might be described as 'next' to China. There was Laos, for one, immediately south from Panxian.

This country of mountains and forests, landlocked between Thailand, Vietnam and China, had become a French protectorate by the end of the 19th century and remained so for over fifty years. After a brief Japanese occupation, France had re-established control, despite the Chinese-backed nationalist movement. But by the time Rose and Alfred first arrived the country had been given a degree of autonomy under its constitutional monarch, as an Associated State of the French Union.

Invited by some Swiss missionaries to work with them among the Chinese in Pakse, Laos, the Bosshardts agree, having first obtained the blessing of their own mission – now renamed Overseas Missionary Fellowship.*

Even so, as Alfred, now in his mid-fifties, put it, 'It was hard to visualise with serenity and detachment starting from scratch again.' The place in which they were to make this start was a provincial town in the south of Laos. As elsewhere in the country, it had a multiracial population, in which the Buddhist Laotians were very much in the majority and the Chinese, with their mixture of

*It changed its name again in 1993, and is now known simply as OMF International.

Taoism, Confucianism and Buddhism, a minority among many others.

A small Laotian Christian church existed but as yet the Chinese were unreached with the Christian message. Having a keen business sense, they often became shopkeepers. And, as the Bosshardts were mightily relieved to learn, their young at any rate were taught Mandarin at school and could therefore speak it well. So at least there was no language barrier between them and the Chinese. Their fluency in French was also a big advantage in terms of easy communication with their Swiss colleagues and when it came to having to fill in official documents.

But culturally, as they quickly realised, the Chinese here were rather different from those in mainland China with whom they had lived and worked for so long. A greater diversity of influences, both Asian and European, had clearly had their effects on Laos and everyone living there. Alfred and Rose became aware of this and did their best to adjust and make friends.

Back in China, they had worn Chinese clothes. But here European-style dress was the norm for the Chinese and so the Bosshardts fitted in accordingly. Next, they began a Sunday afternoon service for the young. Their love for children and Alfred's storytelling gifts quickly came into their own at this enterprise, and all went well, at first.

And then, one day, no one arrived. This, it transpired, was because the children had been forbidden to attend, a rumour having reached the ears of their parents and teachers that the Bosshardts were spying for the French. Alfred could have been forgiven for feeling angry and impatient at yet again having his work and motives as a missionary falsified. But all he wrote was: 'The suspicion had to be lived down.' He and Rose continued to visit and invite people to meetings, but with little result.

Then some young men, sons of local shopkeepers, came to ask whether they could learn English. Alfred was ready to accept the challenge. He took over a small shop front which was to serve as both classroom and chapel. Here daily language classes began. After the lessons the pupils and Alfred would read the Bible, sing and pray. Rose was involved, too, giving a few people French lessons.

A Chinese preacher whom the Bosshardts knew came and joined them for a month of special meetings over the Christmas holiday. His ancestor, sixty-seven generations back, had been Confucius' favourite disciple. Brought up within the Confucian traditions, David Yan had become a Christian and then, believing that God was calling him to preach to the poor, had trained as a minister.

God had used David's talks to touch people's hearts in many places. Rose and Alfred were praying for a similar breakthrough amongst their little congregation.

David was impressed by the way the students sang hymns and seemed familiar with the Bible, and felt hopeful that they would respond well to his talks. But they didn't. As the meetings continued and no one made a commitment to Christ, he grew more and more puzzled and disappointed.

'His ministry was remembered and bore fruit in later years,' Alfred was one day able to write. Meanwhile David resumed his itinerant preaching work until, being offered and accepting a new challenge, he went to Hong Kong to head up the Christian Faith Mission in its care of thousands of under-privileged children in various schools and orphanages.

At about the time that Alfred and Rose took their first home leave from Laos, the country became fully independent from France. But this did not bring peace. Instead civil war broke out between the moderates who had supported the French compromise and the more extreme Communist resistance group, the Pathet Lao.

Back from Manchester and Switzerland, Alfred and Rose celebrated their silver wedding in 1956.

'The twenty or so missionaries who were with us a quarter of a century ago,' Alfred wrote, 'are now scattered throughout the world and a few are with the Lord. What a different China we find today! If a prophet had arisen then to tell us what the years would bring – that China's doors should be closed against us, that we should be working in Laos – how fantastic it would all have seemed! The future was all veiled for us and it still is, but we do take courage as we face another term, for "God is with us".'

A year later, Laos became part of the OMF's new mission field. The Chinese people, though friendly, continued to be unresponsive or at least less than wholehearted towards the Christian message.

Alfred felt very discouraged, but he pressed on with his English classes – sometimes as many as nine a day. He gave the lads English names, and put his whole heart into teaching them both the English language and the Christian faith.

Politically, the situation was still unstable. The coalition government set up in 1957 had quickly collapsed, and three years later a third, right wing, force emerged and set up a pro-Western government.

In this same year, 1960, Rose and Alfred heard the sad news of the death, after a stroke, of Alfred's younger sister, Lily Brunnschweiler. To be far away from loved ones at such a time was not easy. The work in Pakse was not proving easy either, but at last, through one of the students, things began to change for the better.

JOY AND GRIEF

Henry Ly had been brought as a baby by his parents from Vietnam to Laos. They made their home in Pakse and found work there. It was here, too, that Henry as a schoolboy first met Alfred and Rose.

'I went to study French with Auntie Rose in the chapel for about two months,' he wrote. 'From 1953 to 1956 I went to school in Saigon, Vietnam. Then from 1956 to 1962 Uncle Alfred taught me English, the Bible and how to play the organ. Every Monday to Friday, from 7.15 a.m. to 8.30 a.m. he taught me one hour English and fifteen minutes Bible.

'He taught many students, some for a few months, others for one or two years. I probably studied longest with him. All his teaching was free of charge. My class started with six students, but in the last two years I was the only one left in the class, though there were other students at other levels. The students sometimes arrived late, but Uncle Alfred was always very early in the classroom, waiting for our arrival.

'He prepared his Sunday sermon in Chinese. I often helped to write the main topics of his sermon on the blackboard in the Gospel Hall for him. On Saturday he and Auntie Rose always cycled around to invite people to come to the Sunday services.

'Uncle Alfred fasted a few times in a year – sometimes for three or four days. The longest time that I knew of was for about thirteen days. While fasting, he did not eat anything, only drank water. And he continued to teach and work as usual. One day, after finishing my English lesson, he asked, "Does my face look any different?" When I replied that it didn't, he said, "Henry, I don't tell people about this, but I want you to know that I have not eaten anything for eleven days. I have been drinking only water." And he explained to me the reasons for fasting.'

To Alfred's great joy, Henry made a commitment to Christ and wanted to be baptised. His parents forbad this and made him stop attending his lessons. But the young man stuck to his guns and, after a time, his parents allowed him to resume his studies. They were still dead set against his baptism, but at the age of twenty Henry felt he had the right to make his own decisions and so, choosing to obey God rather than man, he was baptised.

'His conversion,' Alfred wrote, 'really marked the beginning of the Chinese church in this place.' Attendances at meetings began to improve and there were more conversions and baptisms, including those of Max, Harold, Oswald and Calvin. Alfred cared for these young people as though they were his own children, rejoicing with them when all went well and weeping when they stayed away or lost their love for God.

Home leave in 1961/2 gave the couple, now in their mid-sixties, a break and change of scene. In a letter written during that time Alfred speaks of an amazing reunion in Manchester with some of the original members of the prayer circle which he had started before going to China. Later to become a monthly CIM prayer meeting, it had kept going for forty years, its membership changing as many left to work as missionaries elsewhere and as new people joined the group.

A further encouragement, soon after the Bosshardts' return to Pakse, was the arrival of new missionary colleagues, Patrick and Ursula Grace and their family. The Graces have many happy memories of the couple they came to know and love as 'Uncle Alfred' and 'Auntie Rose'.

Ursula Grace remembers Rose at that time as a rather petite, quiet-spoken lady, with a sweet smile. Now bespectacled, she wore her white hair tied back in a soft bun. She still spoke English with a slight French accent and the odd French phrase thrown in.

Alfred, also bespectacled, his hair and moustache now grey, was still a good communicator – 'talking' with his hands as well as his good, strong voice – interested in people, well-informed and enthusiastic.

Always having had a great deal in common, Rose and Alfred had grown closer through long companionship and shared affliction, and were more in tune with and complementary to one another than ever.

'Uncle Alfred had a poetic gift,' Ursula Grace remembers, 'and he always wrote a poem for Auntie Rose's birthday or their wedding anniversary – usually on the theme of a rose.

'Every Sunday morning, just before the Chinese service would start, Auntie Rose took out her bike and cycled round all the shops to remind the young men that it was Sunday and the service was about to start and begged them to come along, while Uncle Alfred sat in the chapel playing the harmonium. I wonder how many would have turned up if Auntie Rose hadn't got on her bike!

'Uncle Alfred was someone special, and so was Auntie Rose, and no one will ever be like them. They were a tremendous challenge to us, being so dedicated to God, with such a deep desire to see the Chinese in Pakse coming to know the Saviour they so loved.

'On his way to and from teaching English and chapel Alfred would always stop to give us a running account of who was or wasn't there, and we would always know whether he was discouraged or encouraged. He always said so and was very open about his feelings.

'Their home was always open and welcoming. Auntie Rose enjoyed talking with other women especially, as Alfred's world and work was a man's world.

'Uncle Alfred always had something interesting to talk about. When time allowed for relaxation, he loved doing jigsaw puzzles or collecting stamps. He loved children and they loved him. He could make a jumping mouse out of a handkerchief to the great delight of our children.

'He always got up very early, almost before dawn, and would often read the Bible aloud outside the house because it was lighter there. He liked a good cup of tea – the water always had to be freshly boiled for it and the teapot warmed. He would know if one cheated about either of those things!

'Once, when Uncle Alfred was about to go on home leave, he wanted to take a peacock's tail home with him. A Lao church elder offered to get him one. Sure enough, next day the man arrived with an enormous and very beautiful tail. But the smell! We had visions of him taking the thing on a plane... But, keeping a straight face, he merely asked politely for another tail feather.

'The next day he was brought one that had been properly treated and hence didn't smell. So everyone was happy and no one lost face. He had that sort of way with people.

'Uncle Alfred and Auntie Rose's work bore fruit much later. Harold's parents became Christians – a miracle in view of how opposed they were to their son becoming a Christian. One of the most precious memories we have is of coming back from furlough and walking past Harold's china shop to see his mother sitting outside the shop, busily reading her Chinese Bible. She had made life so difficult for Harold after he became a Christian, but now she was one herself.'

After leaving Laos, Alfred continued to follow events in that country with keen interest. Following years of guerilla warfare, influenced by the conflict in Vietnam, a fragile peace was established through the 1973 Ventiane Agreement. Again a coalition government was set up between the pro-Western faction and the Communist Pathet Lao, later known as the People's Front. Not long afterwards, in 1975, the Communists took total control and Laos became a People's Democratic Republic under the presidency of Prince Souphanouvong.

Most of Uncle Alfred's 'boys' from Pakse, along with 350,000 others, left Laos just before or soon after the Communist take-over. The majority headed for North America, Europe, Australia and

New Zealand. Some went to Thailand where they ended up in refugee camps. The loss of thousands of skilled people, and the adverse effects on the economy of the implementation of Communist principles, finally caused the regime to realise that it would have to modify its approach.

Among those who left Laos was Henry Ly. He went with his family, first of all to Taiwan and then, in 1978, with his wife Mary and their three small children, to Canada. There, in Vancouver, his facility with languages – he spoke at least eight – made him invaluable in his work with refugees, then at the Immigration Centre, and finally, from 1989, in the Foreign Worker Recruitment Unit.

Writing in 1995 from Vancouver, Henry said, 'Some of Uncle Alfred's students became Christians after leaving Laos. One of them is Sidney – he is living in Australia, working for the immigration department. His wife and children are all baptised.' As Ursula Grace commented – the work of Alfred and Rose bore fruit later. But good fruit is often the result of costly sowing and tending.

Alfred left Laos in 1966 – alone. During their last spell of work in Pakse, when both had passed the official retiring age, Rose had a slight stroke. Gradually she got better and worked at recovering her ability to write and speak clearly. Then she developed a liver complaint, which was treated in Saigon. She recuperated with friends who lived in a cooler part of the country. But soon after her return home the heat and humidity began to tell on her, and the doctor advised against her staying in the tropics for much longer.

A farewell Chinese feast was given by Mrs Liu in the missionaries' honour. Too ill to eat much, Rose lay on a camp bed not far from their guests. She thoroughly enjoyed the occasion. But that night and the next day her condition worsened. And in the evening she quietly stopped breathing.

Alfred's acceptance that this, like everything else, came from God's good, loving hand did not lessen his grief. It did, however, keep it free of bitterness and self-pity.

Rose and Alfred had been totally at one in their love and obedience to God, and in their love for and willingness to serve the people to whom they believed he had called them. Through nearly thirty-five years of working as a team, sharing small and great changes and challenges, joys and sorrows, their love for each other had deepened. But it had never been inward-looking, excluding others. Rather, like their love for God, it had helped them to be outgoing and generous.

It was their joint grief that they had had no children. They had not married young, and then there had been Rose's miscarriage and Alfred's captivity and subsequent ill-health during the years when they still might have conceived a child. In the end, for whatever reason, they were childless. But this shared sorrow had the effect of drawing them closer together, deepening their commitment to God and the Chinese people, and channelling the love they could not focus on their own child into all their other relationships and their work.

After Rose's death Alfred was able to continue to be the man she had helped to make him. He never stopped thinking, speaking or writing of her, drawing strength and comfort from the Christian hope of seeing her again one day.

'The Chinese Christians,' wrote Alfred, 'were marvellous. When they knew I wished Rose to be among the Chinese in death as in life, they went out to the new cemetery, six kilometres away, to select a place and make arrangements.'

There were twelve nationalities represented at Rose's funeral. Alfred spoke of her thirty years in China and fourteen in Laos. He continued: 'This is my wife's passport. It was all in order, stamped officially, so that she could pass through Thailand and Italy to Switzerland. There would be no question about her entry there. Now she has gone to another country, a heavenly one, but her papers for that land were prepared when her name was written in the Book of Life. Is your passport for heaven in order?'

The funeral procession walked through the street to the cemetery singing hymns. The students collected money together to pay for all Rose's funeral expenses and there was more money over for Alfred.

The next year a memorial stone was laid on Rose's grave. On it, under a cross, in French and Chinese, were the words, 'For God so loved the world, that he gave his only begotten Son, that whosoever believeth in him should not perish but have everlasting life.'

In October that same year, Alfred was back in England, 'believing,' as he wrote, 'I had said goodbye to the Chinese, now closer and dearer to my heart than even my own countrymen.' He added, cryptically, 'I was wrong.'

Alfred and Rose with Alfred's parents, Heinrich and Marie Bosshardt, probably 1947-48, when Rose and Alfred were on home leave from Panxian not long before Heinrich's death.

Rose in Chinese dress with unidentified friend.

Alfred and Rose on home leave from Panxian 1947-48.

Rose buying vegetables, probably in Panxian, Guizhou, 1941-51.

Alfred rehearsing a choir in Pakse, Laos, where he and Rose worked together from 1951-65.

Rose and Alfred going on home leave from Pakse via Air Lao 1961-62. They had reached retiring age but were asked to return for one last spell of work in Pakse.

A row of shops in Pakse before the Communist takeover in 1975. Note the round rice baskets which held the glutinous rice which was a staple diet. There are also fishing nets, suitcases, kettles, pots and pans. The bicycle was the most common form of transport.

The Bosshardts with six of the Chinese Christians, all in European-style clothes, outside the Chinese chapel in Pakse 1962.

Alfred playing the piano at his wife's memorial service in Pakse in 1966, a year after her death. The words of John 3:16 were carved on her memorial stone in Chinese and French.

MANCHESTER – 1966-1990

BACK TO THE FUTURE

To his immense joy, Alfred found that his return to Manchester did not spell the end of his opportunities to pursue his calling. During his absence Chinese people, many of them young, had been flocking to Britain, to study, train and work.

The vision of making contact with these and other Chinese outside China had been caught by the founders of The Chinese Overseas Christian Mission, under whose auspices the Manchester Chinese Christian Fellowship had been established. Later called the Manchester Chinese Christian Church, it attracted Malaysian, Singapore and Hongkong students.

They met first of all in one another's flats and digs, then in borrowed rooms in City Centre churches. By 1968, in answer to prayer, they were given a small chapel in Moss Side, where numbers grew. When the City Council decided to demolish and rebuild that area, the compensation, plus Christian giving, provided them with purpose-built premises closer to Chorlton.

Alfred arrived in Manchester feeling tired and ill and like a fish out of water. The welcome given to him by the Chinese Church was just what he needed. 'I could do little more than attend their meetings and speak occasionally,' he wrote, 'and then I was asked to be an adviser on their committee. My contribution was modest because of such excellent Chinese leadership, but what joy to see their vigorous witness. They are *my* people.'

Returning to Manchester also brought Alfred the joy of meeting or renewing contact with the Christians who had stood behind him and Rose all through their missionary careers. Union Hall Evangelical Church had been particularly faithful and committed. It had been here that people had gathered to pray for Alfred under threat of death in captivity; and then to welcome the couple home after Alfred's release. Deryck Thompson, whose father Francis had been Union Hall's pastor at the time of Alfred's departure for China, has a particular memory of that happy meeting. For, realising that Alfred was still too weak to get up the stairs to the main hall where everyone was waiting to hear him speak, he carried him there in his arms.

Now, nearly thirty years later, the whole congregation welcomed Alfred with open arms in the metaphorical sense, giving him an honorary place on the church council. He worshipped and attended church gatherings there regularly, and for some years one of the church housegroups met in his home. Deryck, its leader, remembers Alfred as 'an inspiration ... always ready to make a mature contribution, adding to the relaxed fellowship with his warmth, his humour and his love. We were all delighted to be in his home week by week.'

Along with church activities, letter-writing continued to take up much of Alfred's time and energy. His incoming mail from all around the world was vast. Each letter was lovingly and meticulously read, prayed over and responded to. By now about 500 people received his newsletters – two sides of paper, closely typed, packed with up-to-date information about missionary colleagues and national Christians in the Philippines, Hong Kong, Japan, Cambodia, Taiwan, Korea, and, of course, Laos and China.

In one of his newsletters, Alfred wrote:

'In 1919 young Chinese intellectuals first demonstrated in Beijing against the tyranny of the warlords. From that time onwards, Marxism was seriously considered as a practical alternative. "A new China" was the goal held before the minds of young people. Sadly, Christianity, seen through a haze of colonialism, did not seem to provide any solution to the national problems. Later in 1957 Mao announced, "You, young people, full of vigour and vitality are our hope." During the Cultural Revolution (1966-1976) youth went on the rampage, the infamous Red Guards destroying the four "old's" of China's culture, custom, history and education... Disillusion followed the fall of Mao. The reign of the Red Guard is now known as the "lost generation". Since the rise of Deng Xiaoping the atmosphere has changed to one of optimism. Extensive educational reforms are swaying the country and the despised and persecuted intellectuals are reinstated and honoured once more.'

As well as keeping up with reading and correspondence, Alfred found time to work on a second, extended autobiography, which was published by OMF books in 1973 under the title, *The Guiding Hand*. This was also translated into French and German.

But none of this meant that Alfred lived in the past. While still keeping up with old friends and concerns, he gave himself to the present: to life in the land and city of his birth, both much changed during his forty years away from them. By the time he retired Britain had been through a war, nationalised her railways and set up a National Health Service, lost most of her colonies and failed to enter the Common Market.

As well as feeling the effects of what was happening nationally, Manchester was a city in transition, with the added disadvantage of being a prototype industrial city having no comparable models by way of guide or warning.

With the decline in its textile industries, partly due to foreign competition, it was having to diversify, as well as effect a shift away from a manufacturing basis towards the services end of the market.

Worst affected by all the changes were certain inner city areas. These became even more run down as, increasingly, people moved away to find work and better environments elsewhere. At the same time immigrants continued to arrive from Commonwealth countries, only to end up, all too often, in one or other of these areas of deprivation.

Moss Side, where Alfred had lived to young adulthood, had altered greatly, and was to be the centre for various redevelopment schemes over the years. The Baptist Church in particular, where he had come to faith and heard his call to China, declined in the 1970s and was subsequently rebuilt in the hope that a substantial youth work could again be established.

Less affected was Chorlton-cum-Hardy, where Alfred's parents had made their second home and lived out the rest of their lives. By 1966, when Alfred moved in to the little house in Kings Road, Ida had been living on her own there for fifteen years. She was now Alfred's only surviving sister, Lily having died six years earlier.

It was this sister, Lily, with whom Alfred had felt at one in important respects. Like Alfred called to missionary work, she had gone first to the Faith Mission in Edinburgh and then to the island of Islay to pursue her vocation. After marriage to Arthur Brunnschweiler, she had continued to be involved with missionaries and their work, often having them to stay at her home.

David, the oldest of her three children, recalls these missionary visitors with mixed feelings. 'Whilst I liked a few of them very much indeed, I generally found them assertive, even aggressive, which they probably had to be to sustain their vocation,' he wrote, adding, 'My mother always supported them wholeheartedly whatever the circumstance. A very quiet, serious person, always a missionary at heart, she – like my father – was dedicated to the local evangelical church, and was always visiting poor or sick people.'

Lily was greatly missed when she died at the age of sixty-one; chiefly, of course, by her immediate family, but also by the brother and sister who survived her. By the time Alfred returned from Laos, he was sixty-nine and Ida seventy-six. Adjusting to life together was not easy for either of them.

Temperamentally fairly different, their life experiences had diverged considerably. Ida was basically a home bird and, after a long spell of ill health, somewhat emotionally fragile and a bit inclined to be dreamy and disorganised. She was also a very friendly, chatty, sympathetic person, who still thought the world of her missionary brother, and was particularly fond of children. Someone living in the area still remembers Ida making toffee with the neighbours' children. Her liking for cats was also evident.

Alfred had some of the same qualities but he was a more focused person, with a wider and more diverse experience of life, places and people. For these reasons, and because as a man he felt he should, he took the lead in the relationship – just as he had in his marriage. Ida, though upset that Alfred did not share her enthusiasm for cats, seemed to accept her brother's role in their life together. In any case her genuine fondness for Alfred, and his for her, helped them to settle down to a harmonious life together.

But it wasn't to last. After only three years Ida died. Alfred, having now been bereaved of his wife and all the members of his original family, was anchored by his Christian hope.

A year later, in 1970, his brother-in-law moved in with him. Arthur Brunnschweiler had central heating installed in the house and saw to other amenities which must have benefited them both. The two men had very different personalities and ideas – Arthur being a more careful, organised and orderly person than Alfred – and besides, they had long been accustomed to their own ways of doing things. So, while sharing a home, they retained a measure of independence and privacy, treating one another with mutual respect and affection. In their different ways, each was equally committed to the same Christian faith.

After Arthur's death in 1980 from a heart attack, Alfred wrote: 'The beautiful funeral service was conducted by the pastor of Chorlton Evangelical Church. A former pastor spoke feelingly of Arthur's sterling Christian character. Converted as a young businessman in India, he continued to love and serve his Lord during his long life of eighty-seven years... For the last ten years we lived together happily, and naturally I miss his presence tremendously. His three children, David, Frieda and Arthur were present at the funeral, along with six of the grandchildren, other relations and many friends.'

Visits from or to his Manchester-born relatives were special joys in Alfred's life. So too were his contacts with his Swiss family. Yearly highlights for him were long summer holidays in the mountains and meadows of western Switzerland. Over the years the economy of the country had improved, through its thriving tourist industry, hydro-electric schemes, and quality goods, including, still, Swiss watches and clocks.

Although the number of Rose's siblings had obviously been depleted over the years, there were still numerous Piaget cousins, nephews and nieces ready to welcome Alfred at La Côte-aux-Fées. Here, each year, he stayed with Rose's niece Irma, and renewed links with his many friends and supporters at the generous, missionary-minded Free Church from which his wife, and Louisa Köhler before her, had gone to China. It gave him great pleasure to introduce others to the joys of Switzerland and to his Swiss family and friends, and afterwards to take home calendars and chocolates for sharing out.

'The village,' Alfred wrote in 1990, 'is 4,000 feet above sea level and grazing country, so that we had fresh milk, butter and cheese from the very cows we saw from our windows. Most of the vegetables and berry fruits were from our own garden, and as the Swiss are excellent cooks we were well nourished.'

On his way to or from Switzerland, he also regularly visited his many friends at the Chinese Church in Paris. In 1979 he wrote of a delightful incident which occurred during one such visit: 'As I was entering a Chinese restaurant in Paris for a meal, a Chinese lady stepped forward and addressed me by name. She told me she was a refugee from Pakse. Then she added, "I knew your dear wife – she was such a blessing to me – I shall never forget her".'

Returning each autumn, he would get back into the swing of

church and home life. After Arthur's death, he added to his other activities something which gave him virtually a new lease of life. He took in Chinese students as lodgers, two at a time.

'Perhaps my chief memory of Uncle Alfred,' Beatrice Jackson, a friend, was to write later, 'was his keen interest in Chinese young men and the development of the Chinese Christian Church here in Manchester. There was real joy in a young person's conversion and growth in Christ and keen disappointment at any loss of enthusiasm or commitment.

'For years he had two Chinese students living with him. When I appeared to help, mid-morning, he would often tell me what they had said or read or sung at the breakfast table. He was very strong on this time of prayer and Bible reading after breakfast. I used to wonder how they fitted it all in before they left for lectures.

'The programme seemed to be: Uncle Alfred rose at 5 o'clock, read his Bible and prayed, prepared breakfast, woke the boys at 7 o'clock, gave them breakfast at 8 o'clock, sang a hymn for which he played the piano, had a reading with comments, and then prayer with Operation World.*

'He told me laughingly that they often had cake for breakfast – there was no other time to have it! The boys had a meal at University, then a Chinese meal in the evening, so they enjoyed English cake for breakfast. There was usually plenty of cake, anyway, made by a friend.'

Alfred took his new responsibilities very seriously but also thoroughly enjoyed his Chinese lodgers.

'It was fun to have my two Chinese companions with me for Christmas,' he wrote in 1981. 'They were sceptical about Father Christmas but when they found their stockings stuffed with good things on Christmas morning, they changed their minds somewhat!'

---

*A book giving up-to-date information about every country in the world, ed Patrick Johnstone, OM.

GOD'S SURPRISES

Alfred enjoyed giving others surprises – and receiving them himself. Eve Killey, a friend who sometimes came in to cook or serve a meal for Alfred, recalls him saying, often, 'Make it a surprise, Eve!' He prayed for surprises, too, she said. And his prayers were answered.

On his return from Switzerland in 1986, he was amazed by what he found at home. 'Volunteer friends had transformed my house, scrubbed and polished, repapered, painted, carpeted and put down linoleum where necessary. All was gleaming. The kitchen was completely renewed. Praise the Lord for loving friends!'

But there were bigger surprises too, bringing totally unexpected joys: bread cast on the water which now returned to him after many days.

First of all the joy, at long last, of heartwarming news from China. As, tentatively, the country became more open, news concerning the churches and Christians there began to filter through to the West. And the missionaries who had been expelled were overjoyed to learn that, far from dying or being crushed out of existence, Christian fellowships were vigorous and expanding.*

Letters began to get through from some of these. To Alfred's delight, he heard from one and another of the people he and Rose

---

*Since 1977 the growth of the Christian Church in China has been phenomenal. Some researchers have estimated that by 1990 there were between 25 and 50 million Christians there.

had worked among: they remembered the missionaries with affection and wanted to let them know that they were still following Jesus Christ.

In the wake of this came other joys relating to new friendships and challenges. Two people in particular helped to draw public attention to Alfred's experiences during the Long March and give him fresh opportunities not just to tell his story but also to point to God's faithfulness. That they both also became his personal friends was a particular source of added pleasure and gratification to Alfred.

One was Anthony Grey, a British writer. He visited Alfred in 1984 to hear about his experiences and subsequently wrote, 'We had much in common because we had both been victims of political cataclysms in China thirty years apart – Alfred a prisoner for eighteen months of the Long March, myself a two-year prisoner in Peking of the 1960s Cultural Revolution. I was researching a novel covering and linking these events and the book which resulted would have been immeasurably poorer without the illumination he provided.'

The other was Harrison Salisbury, an American historian. While in China in the mid-1980s, doing some detailed research for his forthcoming book on Communism – *The Long March – The Untold Story,* he contacted the Sixth Army General Xiao Ke to ask him for information about the prisoner who had translated some maps for him. Xiao Ke told him the story of Alfred's timely help and asked the writer to convey his greetings to the missionary, if he was still alive.

On learning that he was, both men made contact with Alfred. Harrison sent a copy of *The Guiding Hand* to Xiao Ke, and, after meeting and talking with Alfred, a letter about the visit, enclosing photographs taken at the time.

And so, as a truly amazing outcome of an astonishing train of events set in motion by both Anthony and Harrison, Alfred, the only surviving European prisoner from the Long March, and Xiao

Ke, its oldest surviving general, got in touch with one another and began to exchange greetings, messages and letters.

Alfred never ceased to bubble over with delight at this tying-up of loose ends, which he regarded as one of God's richest surprises for him.

Of course, new contacts bring the possibility of sadness as well as joy, and Alfred was sorry to learn about what had happened to He Long, the colourful Second Army General. Initially fêted as a hero, he had met a sad end during the Cultural Revolution. Accused of behaving like a warlord and associating with Chiang Kai-shek, he had been arrested, tortured and finally, in 1976, murdered by medical means.*

General Xiao Ke grieved deeply for his friend and fellow-commander. He himself had had an extremely tough time during the Cultural Revolution, but had survived it, to enjoy a distinguished career and be held in high esteem by young and old alike. Now in his late seventies, he wanted to show his gratitude for the favour Alfred had done him during the Long March, and also, as far as he could, explain and apologise for the Communists' treatment of missionaries.

'While I was on holiday,' Alfred wrote in 1987, 'I replied to the very friendly letter I had received from General Xiao Ke, whose men had arrested us fifty years ago. It came through the Chinese Embassy, London. On my return, the Embassy got in touch with me and asked me for an interview. Three of their staff came. Among the presents they brought me was a handsome, well-illustrated book entitled *PLA Today*. The Defence Attaché who presented it had written therein: "To Mr Bosshardt, the Old Friend of the Chinese People". In 1934 I was denounced as an imperialistic spy and enemy of the people. What a joy it was to be reinstated, a friend now and no enemy!'

---

*He Long was by then a diabetic. His insulin was withheld and he was given glucose injections.

Appropriate to this incident are some words of Annie Lee. 'My memories of dear Mr Bosshardt – Uncle Alfred – are all very fragrant,' she begins and then remembers in particular: 'Alfred would always tell of his captivity experiences without any bitterness, reminding me of the verse that says: "When a man's ways please the Lord, he maketh even his enemies to be at peace with him".'

Feeling very much at peace with his Embassy visitors, Alfred answered their questions about his time with the Red Army. 'This,' he noted with relish, 'opened up the way for me to testify to God's keeping power.'

A year earlier, in 1986, Alfred had been interviewed both for an article in the *Observer* magazine, which appeared under the title 'Forced March', and for a tape which was subsequently placed in the archives of the Imperial War Museum, London.

Also Fritz Platten, a Swiss official now retired who had once kept the Social Archives in Zurich, had come to see him. Information about Alfred, including the French and German editions of *The Guiding Hand*, had long been arriving at his department. As Fritz's father had died during the Russian Revolution, his personal interest had been aroused by Alfred's experiences in China. So, on his retirement, he had come to England to meet the missionary. Afterwards the two men kept in touch and became friends.

Two years later, in 1988, there was a Channel 4 programme on Alfred, called 'Witness of the Long March', based on an interview with Anthony Grey. In the same year Anthony's novel, *Peking*, was published – 'dedicated with the greatest admiration to Alfred Bosshardt, a true hero of our times'. Also, while filming in China, he presented Xiao Ke, then Deputy Minister of National Defence, with a copy of *The Guiding Hand* dedicated personally by Alfred.

The next year there occurred another astounding event which would strike fresh joy and wonder into Alfred's heart. Having read the translation by his secretary of Alfred's autobiography, the General arranged for it to be translated into Chinese and published in Beijing, retaining in English on its cover the original subtitle *Captivity and Answered Prayer in China*. Furthermore, this translated account of Alfred's story was to be used as a history textbook at Beijing National Defence University which trained young officers for China's People's Liberation Army.

It was also to carry an explanatory foreword written by the General. Courteously, Xiao Ke also invited Alfred to contribute his foreword* too, which was translated and included in the Chinese edition. The General's foreword, translated into English, was incorporated into a new British edition of *The Guiding Hand* published in 1990.

In this unique document,† Xiao Ke graciously admits that the Red Army made mistakes, not least in their attitude to missionaries. Also, significantly, he comes down unequivocally in favour of historical veracity rather than a propagandised version of events.

'At that time I had a bad impression of missionaries,' he writes. 'We considered them invaders of our culture so treated them as we treated landlords, confiscating their property and detaining them for ransom. As time passed, I had more contact with Mr Bosshardt. We had many discussions, and jointly organised recreation programmes for the troops. All this brought us to a better understanding...

'Mr Bosshardt's expertise in translating the French map came at a very crucial moment and solved a big problem for us. Through his translation he became the army's "guide" in Guizhou...

'Mr Bosshardt and other missionaries not only brought their religion to China but also established schools, translated scientific and technological journals, improved cultural awareness and practised charitable works. All these benefited us...

'Although we detained Mr Bosshardt, he held no grudges against us. We should admire his heart and attitude and value our contact with him...

---

*See pages 241-244.
†See pages 234-240 for full text in English.

'We did make some mistakes after the set up of the Communist Party. We did not want to talk about them but it is not right to prevent others from doing so. Those who criticise may have their standpoints, and we must see whether this is the truth…

'History is history and cannot be unilaterally distorted to serve politics. There is only one truth which cannot be altered just to suit the needs of politics… The principle of studying history is to pursue the truth.'

The foreword placed alongside Alfred's account makes fascinating reading, highlighting how people writing about the same events from different viewpoints or faiths will interpret them very differently. Alfred, for example, attributes his release to the will and work of God; Xiao Ke, to the gradual improvement in Communist thought policy. Many Christians would not have a problem with accepting *both* of these on the basis that God's knowledge and activity take account of the freedom, actions and choices of the human beings involved.

The foreword pays tribute very directly to Alfred and other missionaries, but implicitly its writer emerges with credit too. Xiao Ke has been brought up in a culture where loss of face ranks as deeply shameful, something to be avoided at all costs. Yet he admits to having made mistakes; and, in the interests of historical truth, has sanctioned the publication of a book not only highlighting some of these but also interpreting events from a Christian standpoint, in contrast to that of an atheistic Communist.

Whatever influenced Xiao Ke to publish Alfred's book and write as he did in the foreword, he was not alone in casting a critical eye over recent Chinese history and wanting change. All over the country people were pressing for greater honesty internally and greater openness internationally. Alfred rejoiced at these changes and was saddened by the retrograde Tiananmen Square massacre in 1989. Xiao Ke, sometimes known as the 'scholar general', was said to be among those who had been against the use of military force on the student demonstrators.

The decision to use violence in this way set China back and brought tragedy into the lives of many Chinese people. From Vancouver, Henry Ly wrote, 'After the killing of demonstrators in Beijing's Tiananmen Square, the Canadian government has allowed the Chinese students, workers and tourists who do not want to go back to China, to stay in Canada.'

In the same letter he commented, illuminatingly, about Pakse, fourteen years after the Communist take-over of Laos: 'For the last three years the Lao government has not harassed the Chinese businessmen. But almost all the houses look very old... My soya bean milk shop and the two shops next to it have disappeared and the whole block of shops opposite too... During the past fourteen years only about five new houses have been built in Pakse. The old market in the city centre has been torn down and they are building a two-storey concrete market similar to the one in Saigon, but after more than two-and-a-half-years it is still unfinished... There are a lot of motorcycles. Even in the villages people can watch colour television programmes... One of your students is now a chairperson of the Chinese school in Pakse. He went to Bangkok hoping to get donations from the Chinese in Thailand towards repairing the Chinese school.'

Replying to personal letters such as these, and praying for the people and situations they evoked, was still, and would always remain, a high priority in Alfred's life.

A MONTAGE OF MEMORIES

Alfred was back in Manchester for twenty-three years. There were joys and surprises, it's true, but for the most part his life centred around domestic chores, receiving visitors, spending time with his lodgers, dealing with correspondence and attending services, meetings and committees. Did he miss 'the danger and adventure of a missionary's life' which had so appealed to his boyish imagination and which had certainly not been lacking from his experience during the previous forty years? Did he see himself as retired, and enjoy the change of pace, or find it unsatisfying and an unwelcome anticlimax to his life?

A montage of memories helps to answer those questions and evoke something of the spirit of the man during this time.

Beatrice Jackson, who came in to help with shopping and other jobs when Alfred was unwell, remembers:

'His filing system – or, rather, lack of it – was unique, but he knew how to work it. One reason why it took a long time to envelope the letters was that, as we helped him, so many personal histories of the people to whom the letters were going had to be told, and indeed it was interesting.'

'One day he was very tired and not very well but it was Friday and the Chinese church had its prayer meeting that day. I asked him, "Are you going to the prayer meeting?" – hoping he would not. He merely answered firmly, "It's my duty." Typical! Always duty first.

'Sunday dinner, he told me, was an English traditional meal cooked by him. He said his boys – his Chinese lodgers – enjoyed it.

This, of course, was between morning service at Union Hall and the 3 p.m. service at the Chinese Church.

'Manchester city streets are illuminated at Christmas and it seemed to be the ritual that he be driven round to see them.

'He had many visitors in the afternoons – after his siesta, when his best china was brought out and a very nice cup of tea made. "China?" the boys sometimes would exclaim and he would explain the difference between China and china.

'I was in the house once, making tea for everybody when he was being interviewed for one of the programmes that were made about him. I was amazed at his fortitude, memory and patience as he was plied with questions. He was very tired but so willing and interesting.

'I accompanied him one year to Switzerland where he spent his annual two to three months with Rose's family and friends. It was a great pleasure for me to see the village of La Côte-aux-Fées and meet the people who loved him. As soon as he arrived, his papers for writing and books for reading were laid out on the table.

'The memory of his dear wife was always with him and I was taken to see her memorial stone in the small, beautifully-kept village cemetery.'

Margaret Hodgkinson, whose husband John was pastor to the Chinese Church in Manchester for fifteen years, adds her memories of the man affectionately known as 'Uncle':

'In old age in Manchester, Uncle loved to have visits from a young Chinese student who played the violin. As he played, Uncle would accompany him on the piano. Union Hall asked this student to play his violin at the church for a musical evening and he persuaded Uncle to accompany him on that occasion. Only then did people realise what a good pianist he was: in his mid-eighties he was playing in public in England for the first time!

'At the Chinese church one evening he told us he had had burglars in the house. Fortunately they had not taken many things or caused chaos, but it was a worrying thing to happen to such an elderly man. I drove him home after that evening's meeting, walked to the front door with him, and waited while he unlocked it and stepped inside. As he did so he called out, "Hello, burglars!" in a clear voice, then turned to me with a chuckle and said, "You see, they may come back."

'He read the Bible avidly – he had a well-used copy of every English translation, all marked with red pen throughout, an indication that he read through the whole Bible, then bought a different translation and started again. He also had his Chinese and French Bibles, and every morning used some Bible-reading notes in French in order to keep up his reading and spoken fluency. Rose had taught him French from the time of their marriage and he always used it in Switzerland. Each day he translated these French Bible notes into English in his desk-size diary.

'He cut out photos of all OMF missionaries as they appeared in OMF prayer diaries and kept them together so he could see their faces as he prayed every day. By breakfast time, when he prayed with his Chinese student lodgers, including intercession for all parts of the world, he had already had several hours of prayer and Bible reading.

'His birthday being January 1st, it was the custom for the church, at the end of our watch-night service on December 31st, as the clock struck midnight, to carry in his huge birthday cake, made by Chinese church members, and sing "Happy Birthday" to him. After blowing out the candles and cutting the first slice, he would read the Psalm of his age. I remember the impact of Psalm 92 in 1989: "They will still bring forth fruit in old age. They will stay fresh and green." We teased him that Psalm 119 might be a little tiring when he reached that age!'

Judith Gabler who did some cleaning for Alfred and was initially wary about working for someone who had been a missionary, writes: 'To my surprise, I found him to be a charming and dear old man, with a wonderful sense of humour, sometimes a little impatient, which I felt was due to frustration at not being able to hear too well and move around as he would have wished.

'His house was an Aladdin's Cave of lovely pieces of furniture, ornaments and pictures, together with some bric-a-brac sent him by children and from people in China and around the world. Books and papers were scattered everywhere, making real cleaning impossible, but he always seemed happy with my efforts.

'I was with him for around two years and I considered him to be a friend. Later, after he left Manchester, we wrote regularly to each other and I visited him once in Tunbridge Wells. He never criticised but gave practical advice.'

Edith Sutcliffe was one of a little team of women who came in regularly to give Alfred various forms of practical help:

'He was nice – I liked Alfred. The way he nursed his sister, after she was ill – it was marvellous. He had a keen sense of humour, too.

'He was always very particular about his meals. There had to be a clean table cloth and his nice pots. If there were only the two of us eating, he'd still want it done properly.

'I've made some good friends through Alfred. I often went to La Côte-aux-Fées with him. His wife's family were lovely, always so welcoming. He always had to take his own typewriter and of course all his pills – ever such a lot of them, and we would count them all out when he was getting ready to go. There was a typewriter out there he could have used, but no, he had to have his own. Even though it often had to be mended after being thrown around on the journey.

'He liked nothing better than getting mail. He used to wait for the postman to come, and if there wasn't a letter he'd get really upset. He used to spend hours and hours writing and answering letters.

'He just loved flowers in the house. Any excuse – he could remember anybody's birthday, all the dates. He had an apple tree in the garden and he used to hack pieces off it so that he could have the blossoms in the house. Then he used to wonder why he had no apples on his trees!

'He couldn't throw anything away. He never bought any clothes.

He always had what people gave him. His niece in Switzerland, Irma, asked me to clear his wardrobe out and get something for the moths. It took us all day to clean out this wardrobe. And after all that, we didn't throw one thing out. Whatever I said about anything, he wouldn't throw it out. So it all went back in. He didn't like wasting anything.

'I remember the day the film producer Aubrey Singer came to discuss making a programme about him. Alfred was so tired, he said he couldn't be bothered to see him, when I told him there was a man from the TV at the door. But I knew if I could just get him talking about China, it'd be all right. And it was. He just talked and talked.'

Chee Yan Chow and Sau Wai Wong were two of Alfred's student lodgers. The former, now a chartered accountant in Singapore, writes:

'The news of Uncle Alfred's death momentarily stunned me. But I was much comforted when I recalled that he once said: "I desire to depart and be with Christ which is better by far."

'Being a young Christian, I was deeply influenced by Uncle Alfred. He provided me with a Christian role model of faithfulness in prayer. His personal discipline was exemplary. He would sleep early and wake up very early to pray every day. I remember vividly how Alfred insisted that we, the sometimes reluctant companions, should, every day, read some verses from the Bible and pray for one country and one missionary. Then we would sing a hymn accompanied by Uncle Alfred as the pianist, before we took our leave to attend the day's activities.

'I fondly remember Alfred for his warm heart that overflowed with affection and bubbly joy. He visibly radiated the love of God and was much loved by the members of the Manchester Chinese Christian Fellowship.

'Now, in my late thirties, I sometimes wonder how I would like to lead my life when I retire. I would very much like to emulate Uncle Alfred – stay active, prayerful, faithful and be surrounded by friends.

'To me Uncle Alfred is a living testimony of this verse: "We do not lose heart. Though outwardly we are wasting away, yet inwardly we are being renewed day by day."'

Sau Wai works with Shell, now in Sarawak, Malaysia, but earlier in The Hague, Holland. He wrote:

'Alfred's love of God and devotion to God's work were most inspiring to me.

'Uncle Alfred was a kind man but also someone who showed great strength of character and rectitude. He had a good sense of humour and was very disciplined.

'He loved music and taught me to appreciate Handel's *Messiah*, and Bach's *Christmas Oratorio*. He consistently prayed for my family. My parents, who met Uncle Alfred twice, were deeply touched by his love for the Lord.

'He was my close friend and also, by his life, my teacher. I am most thankful to the Lord for the privilege and honour of knowing Uncle Alfred Bosshardt.'

Chor Hin Ong, a student who later became a pastor of the Chinese Fellowship in Manchester, said:

'I remember meeting, in 1966, this very unassuming gentleman, with his wonderful Einstein moustache. He had a warm strong handshake: as he shook someone's hand, he would also draw them towards him. And he had a twinkle in his eye, and a smile which made a person feel really welcome.

'Mr Bosshardt had a lot to teach us about prayer. Prayer meetings were different without him. He spoke once or twice about prayer to us, but it wasn't through words that he taught us about prayer. He prayed and lived a life of faith and prayer. And by contact with him we learnt what prayer in faith meant.

'As a fellowship, we learnt from him how to pray together, asking for what we wanted God to do in us. Looking back now, I'm amazed at how we, as quite a small group, experienced God doing great things for us. And I believe that was because Mr Bosshardt had taught us about bringing everything to God in prayer.

'There was nothing austere or dour about Mr Bosshardt's spirituality. He was a man of warm humanity and great personal charm. He was also a cultured person, someone who loved classical music, especially Bach and Handel. And one of the highlights of our visits to him would be to gather round the piano or his old organ and sing a few songs.

'He had practical skills, too, as he lived with his sister and looked after her and the house and did the shopping and cooking, with help from his friends when he wasn't well.

'He lived simply with very few personal luxuries, surrounded by his books and the many letters received from his friends all around the world.

'For a man of his age he had a very lively mind and he kept himself extremely well-informed about current affairs in China, never being judgmental or critical about what was going on, but always showing great interest in and love for the people there.

'It was remarkable how he fitted in. He was so young at heart and carefree, in a way. We never saw him as an old man among us. He was simply Mr Bosshardt and he joined in almost all our activities: dressing up as Father Christmas and giving presents to the Sunday School children; getting involved in sketches at houseparties; joining in games at coffee evenings for new students; going carol singing with the young people.

'Consequently, we, as Chinese people, didn't ever think of him as a white Western missionary. In fact sometimes he was more Chinese than some of us. I remember a dinner we had to celebrate the Chinese New Year. Mr Bosshardt brought his own chopsticks to this, and was rather disappointed that everyone else was using spoons and forks. He really felt at home, comfortable, doing Chinese things with Chinese people.

'Mr Bosshardt wanted to win as many Chinese as he could for Jesus Christ, but he wasn't just interested in someone's soul. He also wanted to befriend people.

'Mr Bosshardt didn't keep boring people to death with his

experiences in China. In fact, sometimes he was quite reticent about what he had been through. He would only talk about it if there were good reasons for doing so. He never gave the impression that he lived in the past, because he was always enjoying the present and looking forward to new things in the future.

'After his sister Ida had died, some of us went round to call on him. He welcomed us in and we found that, far from being subdued or sad, he was quite chirpy. But we gave him our condolences, anyway.

'Then he asked, "Do you want to see her?" And he took us into the lounge where his sister's body was lying in an open coffin. We never expected anything like that, because although we were Christians, we were also Chinese, and in China there are all kinds of taboos about dead people.

'I think Mr Bosshardt was well aware of that, as he went across to his sister and touched her cheek, and said, "Doesn't she look peaceful? She's safe with Jesus now." Then we sang a hymn with the words, "When we all get to heaven", and had a prayer.

'We were so moved by his confidence and joy that his sister was with Jesus and that death was not the victor. When we sang, it wasn't, "*If* we get to heaven" but, "*When* we get to heaven". What happened that evening was an unforgettable object lesson about the fact that for the Christian death holds no terror.

'I thank God for Mr Bosshardt's faith in God, his love for the Chinese people, his humour and humanity, his friendship and kindness to me and to many Chinese people in Manchester.'

And finally this, from Albert Pope, former pastor and elder of Union Hall Evangelical Church:

'Alfred was a man of the church. He never failed to report back. He recognised not only the responsibility that the church had towards him, but also his responsibility towards them. He always kept the church informed about what was happening and what God was doing.

'The primary Sunday School became very involved in Alfred and

Rose's missionary work. This meant that over the years several hundred children heard about God's work in China and were encouraged to pray for it: an interaction that must have enriched and benefited the young people as well as "their" missionaries.

'Writers, media people and many others, came to Alfred to learn of his experiences on the Long March. But the attention didn't go to his head. He used everything as an opportunity to share with people the love, reality and faithfulness of his God.'

From all these reminiscences, Alfred emerges winsomely with all his basic characteristics intact. Certainly he sometimes feels his age, particularly when illness strikes. But a disillusioned and dispirited has-been he is not! The picture, rather, is of someone pursuing his calling with the same enthusiasm and commitment as he has always shown; loving and trusting God more than ever; relating to others as well as ever; and still enjoying life and ready to see its funny side.

KENT – 1990-1993

THE LAST MILE

'The longest mile is the last mile home' — a saying that perhaps echoed Alfred's feelings at times during the last three years of his life.

At the age of ninety-three, he became very ill. Friends rallied round but finally came to the conclusion that it would be best for him to have full nursing care at the home for retired CIM and OMF missionaries in Pembury, Tunbridge Wells, Kent. He did not share their opinion. In the end he agreed reluctantly, hoping that the move south would be temporary and that he'd soon be able to return to his old life, home and friends in Manchester.

'I'm afraid,' wrote Edith Sutcliffe, 'they didn't get a good idea of what Alfred was like at the nursing home. Not at first anyway. He didn't want to go. He wanted to be up in Lancashire, because he just liked the Chinese church and the people in it and in his own church, and he missed them all.'

The medical diagnosis was cervical cord infarction, which meant, in simple terms, that Alfred had almost no movement from the neck downwards. In this condition, he arrived at Cornford House in March 1990. There, straightaway, the doctor, physiotherapist and staff began an intensive exercise programme, involving Alfred's whole body, including each finger and toe joint.

After six weeks he regained some movement in his hands. With more gradual improvement, he was able to feed himself and even turn the pages of his Bible and other books. His next ambition was to be able to stand. This he managed, with support. But though he could move his legs a little, he was never able to walk again.

Physically limited, Alfred still had his faith, his strong character and his mental faculties. And it wasn't long before he grew to know and like the staff at Cornford House and to appreciate their devoted care. On good days he would call them princesses. And many of them came to regard him with affection and admiration, too. Jean Welch, who with her husband Bernard took over the running of the Home not long after Alfred's arrival, wrote, 'Mr Bosshardt really was a very special man of God, and we counted it a privilege to care for him.'

He loved having visitors – and there were many of these, for friends and relatives did not fail him in his time of weakness and need. Some travelled enormous distances just to be with him for a short time.

For his second Christmas at Cornford House, Sau Wai Wong came over from Holland, arriving on Christmas Eve and staying until after lunch on Boxing Day. 'My dear niece Frieda sent a cooked roast duck, so we fared very well,' Alfred wrote.

A few Manchester friends even took their annual holidays locally so as to be able to spend more time with him. Many Chinese people came to visit, but also others from within and beyond Britain.

One visitor, Anthony Grey, found Alfred as indefatigable as ever, determined to regain the use of his arms and legs and return to Manchester. 'I'm a prisoner of my own body for the moment,' Alfred told him. 'But I won't give up the fight. Perhaps this is another test – perhaps there is some reason for it.'

Aubrey Singer also came. He and Anthony Grey brought Alfred a television and music centre which was easy to operate and a great source of delight to him; it was their wish that this should be donated to Cornford House after Alfred's death.

Jung Chang, author of the classic biography *Wild Swans*, called in with her husband, the writer Jon Halliday. They took photographs of Alfred which Jung Chang promised to show to Xiao Ke on her coming visit to China.

'Do you have a message for the General?' she asked.

Quick as a flash, he responded, 'Ask him if he's still reading the

Bible that I gave him' – a reference to a Bible sent to him in 1991. Jung Chang responded with a delighted chuckle. That, she commented, was exactly the sort of message that she would have expected from Alfred.

Writing of this visit in 1993, Alfred said, 'Dr* Jung Chang, who was a very young Red Guard in the Cultural Revolution of the 1960s, now lives in London and is married to the English writer Jon Halliday. Following the success of *Wild Swans*, Dr Chang has been commissioned to write a biography of Mao Zedong that will be published in Britain and America. She visited me with her husband to gather first-hand material about the Long March and I very much enjoyed recalling details for them. They stayed several hours, and I was told later that they were very pleased indeed with what they learned and were very surprised at the clarity of my recollections.'

To all new visitors, Alfred would point out the photograph of Xiao Ke which hung on his wall. Then, with eyes twinkling and his open, engaging smile and the occasional infectious giggle, he would proceed to tell them the amazing story of how contact had been renewed between them, and of the letters, greetings, gifts and photographs that they had exchanged since his one-time enemy had become his friend.

Referring to Xaio Ke, he said, 'He'd given up a life of ease to face hardship and danger because in his teens he had read the writings of Marx and Lenin. He was very confident then that their ideology could solve China's problems. I told him that I'd been won over early in my life by the "revolutionary" teachings of Jesus Christ. I'd chosen the Holy Bible through which to work for the uplift of mankind…

'When I answered the General's first letter, I told him that I was still as confident as ever that my faith was right and justified. I asked him whether he felt the same about his belief in communism – but he hasn't replied to that point yet.' Right to the end, Alfred held

---

*After leaving China in 1978, Jung Chang went to York University from which she obtained a PhD in Linguistics.

true to his first and greatest love, but most people, if not everyone, found his singlemindedness disarming rather than abrasive.

His great love was still the Bible. When he was unable to read, he listened to parts of it being read on tape. And after a lifetime of prayer, talking to God was as natural as breathing; the presence of God a moment by moment reality.

Music was as important to him as it had always been. Jean and Bernard Welch often heard him joining in the hymn-singing coming from the lounge, the room next door to his, in which the more able-bodied residents gathered for meetings; or singing along with one of his music cassettes; or even having an impromptu sing-song with one or other of his visitors, making a joyful noise that echoed all along the Home's ground-floor corridor.

Letters were a continuing joy in his life. His post was still very heavy and friends would come in to help him send out replies, taking dictation from him and typing out dozens of letters each week.

He still enjoyed his meals. There was a fridge in his room, full of his favourite foods sent by many friends, some of them overseas. Meat, cheese, butter, biscuits, chocolate, especially coffee creams, were particularly relished.

Alfred came to accept that he would never return to his own home back in Manchester, and in 1991 he gladly gave the little house to the Manchester Chinese Christian Church. Its new Chinese pastor and his family moved in, and their home is a constant reminder to them and the whole Chinese Church of Alfred's devotion to God and to them.

Alfred still thought, spoke and wrote a great deal of Rose. His letters often referred to anniversaries connected with her or related treasured memories of her. Her photograph hung on his wall – her serene face and gentle smile reminding him of shared past happiness and beckoning him on to perfect joys which he was certain she was now experiencing and which he looked forward to sharing with her one day.

Meanwhile, like all human beings, Christian believers or not,

Alfred was not exempt from the limitations and pains of old age. Indeed, what he had been through for the sake of his faith and calling brought him, in some respects, added burdens.

Latterly he thought and talked more of the Long March and, at times, memories which distressed and disturbed him would surface, rather than those which would have cheered and comforted him. Suddenly finding himself re-experiencing a moment of trauma, he might cry out, 'Two men have jumped out on me and I can't do anything.'

'Yes, but isn't it wonderful, Alfred, that God delivered and kept you safe through all that?' With such gentle, soothing reminders from the staff member on hand, Alfred's panic would subside and peace return.

There was talk, in 1993, of the Xian Film Studio making a film based on *The Guiding Hand*. But Alfred did not live long enough to hear the outcome of this. He died at the age of ninety-six, from bronchitis, in his room at Cornford House.

Xiao Ke and other Chinese officials sent messages of sympathy to his family.* And at packed memorial services in Manchester and Kent family and friends gathered to celebrate his life and pay tribute to his faith and character. But the emphasis, as he would have wished, was on God's constant and unfailing presence, guidance and faithfulness.

For he had never ceased to assert,

'I've always believed I was led along a path that was prepared for me. I always felt I had the comfort of God's promise never to leave me nor forsake me.'

Words which should, at the very least, in the context of this man and his story, give considerable pause for profound thought.

---

*See pages 245-246.

Alfred playing the piano at the home of his niece Irma Piaget at La Côte-aux-Fées, Switzerland, August 1983. Henry Ly, the first of Alfred's students in Pakse, Laos, to become a Christian, is standing beside him.

Jung Chang, author of Wild Swans, *and General Xiao Ke in Beijing, March 1993. The General and Jung Chang are looking at a map of China. The General is indicating where he met Alfred, near Jiuzhou, Guizhou in 1934.*

Alfred outside his Manchester home with friends where he lived first with his sister Ida, then with his brother-in-law. From 1980 he began taking in Chinese lodgers.

Alfred holding the Chinese edition of The Guiding Hand *which Xiao Ke had asked his secretary to translate into Chinese. Xiao Ke wrote the foreword to the Chinese edition which was translated into English and included in a new enlarged English edition in 1990.*

AUTHOR'S POSTSCRIPT

In Alfred and Rose's time, missionaries were largely white, Western and from the richer more developed countries of the world. For this reason, rightly or wrongly, Christianity and its missionary delegates tended to be seen by some as part and parcel of Western imperialism which was all too often power-hungry, greedy, exploitative and racist. As human beings, missionaries are as prone as anyone else to be sinful in those or any other ways. But as human beings becoming changed by the love, power and Spirit of God, they want to do good and not harm, but know that they are flawed and are willing to admit mistakes, learn and change, as they pass on, through words, action and life, the Christian message.

Like the best of the 'old-fashioned' missionaries, Alfred and Rose's words, actions and life were 'all of a piece'. They loved the people they worked amongst, opened their hearts and homes to them, identified with them, adopted many of their customs and learnt their language. They wanted to win them for God, not for Western civilisation. Unconsciously, they would have conveyed something of their own culture and preferences, but on that charge none of us is exempt, whatever our profession, wherever we go, and whether we are aware of it or not.

Like all missionaries of that era, the Bosshardts' predominant emphasis was on evangelisation. But, again like the best missionaries of all eras, they responded compassionately to people's other needs. For example, Alfred and Rose and their missionary colleagues helped famine victims and did their best to get the authorities to see their plight and take action on their behalf.

They would not have seen their actions as an aspect of what is sometimes called 'holistic mission' – reaching out in compassion to the whole person and fighting for greater justice and equality in society. But in responding as whole people to whole people, sharing whatever good things they had as well as the good news with those they lived amongst, they were in fact being holistic.

The best missionaries, too, were fellow-workers with the people to whom they were 'sent', serving rather than lording it over them, not fostering dependency but being willing to work themselves out of a job, creating a climate in which people matured and were able to take over responsibility for themselves. Alfred and Rose, along with many of their missionary colleagues, had these sorts of attitudes and agendas.

Cross-cultural mission is now recognised to be not just from the West to the rest but from all nations to all nations going in all directions. Alfred did not see the pattern he followed as being set in concrete. Speaking of China and the Chinese, he wrote,

'The future may be with young Chinese Christians, scattered over the face of the whole globe, who one day may join the tourists and businessmen to carry out Christ's great commission to their own people. Stephen Wang, founder of the Chinese Overseas Christian Mission, said, "If China is to be evangelised, it must be by the Chinese."'

Of course Alfred's outlook on life, faith, missionary work, and everything else was influenced by the culture and climate in which he was born and brought up and in which he lived and worked. But he was not tied to it, because he had a point of reference by which he was able to judge it and a power by which he could, where necessary, be set free to march to the music of a different drummer. He was a man of his time in some ways while transcending it in others: in the world, but not of it.

Human and hence imperfect like everyone else, he was still 'a lovely man'. But not 'lovely' as in soft and cosy or easygoing and tolerant. Lovely as in being full of true love for God and others; love that brings delight and joy, but also requires self-discipline, sacrifice and integrity – refusing the easy way out, of negativity, self-pity and resentment – taking up the cross daily and following Jesus through suffering, persecution and ultimately through death.

Now, after his long march, he has arrived, he is home. With God, above all, and then also with his beloved Rose, and other family members and friends, perfectly healed and whole, enjoying every minute of worshipping and serving God. Within a growing company of redeemed people from all nations, some of whom are there now or will be there one day because a boy from Manchester responded to the call to tell the Chinese people the good news of Jesus.

APPENDIX

Alfred Bosshardt's personal chronology within a wider context

PERSONAL	GENERAL
1893	Birth of Mao Zedong
1894 Birth of Rose Piaget Birth of Frieda Bosshardt	
1897 Birth of Alfred Bosshardt	Queen Victoria's Diamond Jubilee
1898 Birth of Lily Bosshardt	
1899	Unrest, riot, rebellion throughout China
1900	Boxer atrocities against foreigners – sanctioned by Empress Dowager – many missionaries murdered
1901 Alfred's parents become committed Christians; Bosshardts worship at Moss Side Baptist Church, Manchester	
1905	Hudson Taylor dies (b. 1832)
1906 Alfred becomes committed Christian	
1907 Alfred called to China	
1911	Manchu Empire overthrown China a republic in name – still under warlords First World War starts
1914 Alfred apprenticed to engineering Alfred baptised	

1917 Alfred joins Union Hall Mission, later Union Hall Evangelical Church, Manchester	Lenin comes to power
1918 Alfred opts for Swiss nationality	First World War ends Marxist study groups attract intellectuals searching for new ideology for China
1920-25 Rose to China – language study and work in Yangzhou, Tongzhou and Guiyang Alfred in training for CIM	Mao Zedong becomes committed Marxist
1921	Formation of Chinese Communist Party (CCP)
1922 Alfred to China	Communists ally briefly with Government/Kuomintang/Nationalists
1923 Frieda dies	
1922-24 Alfred learning Chinese in Zhenjiang and working in Chongqing and Jiangjin	Joint Communist and Nationalist forces under Chiang Kai-shek. Communists train peasants
1924 Alfred in Zunyi Lily marries Arthur Brunnschweiler	
1925 Rose in Zhenyuan	Mao Zedong – helping to train peasants, urges revolution through countryside – ignored
1926 Alfred – famine, orphanage work, typhus – in Zunyi	Chiang Kai-shek's joint forces (KMT and CCP) go on Northern Expedition against warlords
1927 Rose – home leave	Chiang attacks and slaughters many Communists in Shanghai Communist insurrections
1928-29 Rose returns – meets Alfred again	Chiang completes his Northern Expedition
1929	Mao's forces move to Jiangxi

1930 Rose and Alfred – engaged
Alfred – brief home leave

1930-33

1931 Rose and Alfred marry – work
in Zhenyuan
Death of Papa Piaget

1933

1934 Alfred and Rose captured by
6th Red Army
Haymans and Grace Emblen
captured
Rose, Rhoda Hayman and
children released and reach
safety, Grace released and safe
John and Betty Stam beheaded
6th Red Army joins 2nd Front
Army
Alfred and Arnolis sentenced
as 'enemy of the people'

1935 Arnolis released in November.
Alfred continues with Red
Army

Mao creates Jiangxi soviet
Urban activities of Communists less
successful – forced to withdraw to
countryside
Nationalists launch five Encirclement
Campaigns against Communists –
four repulsed
5th – 750,000 Nationalist troops
prove too much for Communists
Japan invades Manchuria – while
Nationalists are diverted,
Communists achieve some successes
Truce with Japan – Chiang able to
attack Communists again
Red Army suffers heavy losses while
blockaded at Jiangxi but breaks
through to begin fighting retreat to
Shaanxi – known collectively as Long
March but involving several armies
and routes
Communists travel through south-
west China – guerilla style –
spreading propaganda and gaining
support from peasants and others

Mao made senior leader at Zunyi
Conference in January
Clashes within Communist Party
leading to division of forces
First marchers reach Shaanxi
September
Second marchers with Mao arrive
October

1936 Alfred released – Easter *The Restraining Hand* published Alfred and Rose to Switzerland and England	Last marchers arrive October Mao's leadership established – starts regrouping for overthrow of Nationalists and Communist conquest of China
1937	Japan attacks deep into China Anti-Japanese War – KMT-CCP alliance
1938 Alfred and Rose in Switzerland, Belgium, England	
1939-40 Alfred and Rose in U.S.A. and Canada	Second World War starts
1940 Alfred and Rose return to China	
1941 Alfred and Rose in Panxian	Collapse of KMT-CCP alliance – clashes and civil war
1945	Second World War ends Japanese surrender
1946	KMT-CCP civil war
1947-48 Rose and Alfred on home leave – celebrate Rose's mother's 90th birthday	
1948 Alfred's father dies Rose's mother dies	Communist victories
1949	Mao Zedong proclaims People's Republic of China Communists start taking over country Chiang Kai-shek flees to Taiwan
1950	Communists take over Panxian – whole of mainland China 'liberated' by Communists China enters Korean War Laos semi-autonomous as an Associated State of the French Union

1951 Alfred's mother dies Missionaries expelled – Alfred and Rose leave Panxian, China and go to Pakse, Laos	Campaign in China against counter- revolutionaries
1954	Laos full independence from France but civil war between moderate pro- French group and extreme Communist resistance group – Pathet Lao
1955-56 Alfred and Rose on home leave	
1956 Alfred and Rose's silver wedding	
1957 Laos officially becomes an OMF field	Coalition government established in Laos – soon collapses
1960 Lily dies	Third right-wing force emerges, sets up pro-Western government in Laos
1960-63 Henry, Calvin, Max, Harold and Oswald become Christians and are baptised	
1961-62 Alfred and Rose on home leave	
1962 Patrick and Ursula Grace come to live in Pakse	In Laos, attempt to combine right, left and neutral elements under Prince Souvanna Phouma but more conflict follows
1965 Rose dies	
1966 Alfred returns to Manchester – home with Ida	In China, Mao's Cultural Revolution starts – Red Guards reign of terror
1969 Death of Ida	Cultural Revolution formalised Mao's health declines Zhou Enlai in power
1970 Arthur Brunnschweiler moves in with Alfred	
1971 Arnolis Hayman dies	Some rapport between China and USA
1972	Nixon's visit to China

1973 *The Guiding Hand* published	In China, Zhou returns Deng Xiaoping to power – opposed by radicals
	In Laos, Ventiane Government and Pathet Lao agree to a ceasefire
	Fragile coalition between pro-Western faction and Pathet Lao
1975	Communists take power in Vietnam
	Pathet Lao in Laos becomes very active – take over city after city
	Laos renamed Lao People's Democratic Republic
	Communist rule established – thousands leave and economy suffers
1976	In China, Tiananmen Square – demos. Protest crushed – Deng blamed
	Chiang, Mao and Zhou die
	Gang of Four arrested
1977	Deng back in power
1978	Mao's 'class struggle' abandoned
	China committed to 'reform and openness' with modernisation and expansion of foreign trade
1979	In Laos, government realises need to modify/reform Communist policies
	Gang of Four sentenced
1980 Arthur Brunnschweiler dies Alfred takes in Chinese lodgers	Mao criticised moderately
1982	Deng's policies affirmed
1984 Article about Alfred and Long March in Beijing paper	Communists plan to reform China's economy and allow free enterprise
Harrison Salisbury meets Xiao Ke and speaks of Alfred	Thousands of Chinese students go to the West, especially USA
Anthony Grey visits Alfred – also Aubrey Singer	Phenomenal growth of church in China

1986 Harrison Salisbury brings greetings from Xiao Ke
Observer article on Alfred
Imperial War Museum tape interview with Alfred
Alfred hears from Christians in Zunyi
Alfred visited by Franz Platten, ex-keeper of Social Archives, Zurich

1987 Exchange of letters between Xiao Ke and Alfred
Alfred is sent book from Xiao Ke via Chinese Embassy – *PLA Today*, dedicated to him as 'an old friend of the Chinese people'

1988 Anthony Grey gives Xiao Ke copy of *The Guiding Hand* – publishes novel, *Peking,* inspired by Alfred's story
TV Channel 4 programme on Alfred

1989 Xiao Ke has *The Guiding Hand* translated into Chinese and writes foreword – invites Alfred to write one too

Students have pro-democracy demos in Tiananmen Square – fired on by troops

1990 New edition of *The Guiding Hand* published with Xiao Ke's foreword in English
Xiao Ke's secretary adapts *The Guiding Hand* for TV film
Alfred becomes ill – leaves Manchester for Kent nursing home
New edition of *The Guiding Hand* published with Xiao Ke's foreword in English

Some researchers estimate the number of Christians in China as between 25 and 50 million

1991 Alfred interviewed for Italian TV programme	
1992	Increasing liberalisation in China and decline of hardliners
1993 Jung Chang and Jon Halliday visit Alfred Alfred dies Memorial services held in Manchester and Kent Messages of sympathy from Xiao Ke and others	
1995 Xiao Ke's film of Long March scheduled for release – August	

Copy of a Minute Passed by the China Council at the One Hundred and Seventy-ninth Session Held in Shanghai on June 10, 1936

THE RELEASE OF
MR A. HAYMAN AND MR R. A. BOSSHARDT

With a sense of profound thanksgiving to the Lord the news of Mr Bosshardt's release was received in Shanghai on April 14th and a song of praise went around the world as the information that the captive had been liberated was cabled to the main home centres of the Mission. The China Council desire to place on record a grateful acknowledgement to Mr Hermann Becker who, with persistent hope in God, had for more than twelve months sought by every available means to give succour to our brethren, Messrs Hayman and Bosshardt, and on behalf of the Hunan Provincial Authorities to negotiate terms for release, refusing to be turned from his purpose by disappointments or delays, by his messengers following up the Communist forces from place to place and with resourceful skill leaving no means untried which might be blessed to the end in view. After Mr Hayman was released last November, and Mr Bosshardt still detained, his efforts were resumed, and the captors followed though Kweichow into Yunnan. As all human plans were exhausted, and everything staked on one last effort to reach the leaders in their camp with supplies and medicines for a final settlement, the hand of the Lord intervened and the 'iron gate' opened of its own accord. The fact that Mr Becker sustained a broken arm through a motor bus accident, which was probably the way the Lord took to preserve his life from an ambuscade, did not deter him from his quest, and his tirelessness in all this labour of love will be a lasting memory.

The Council also desire to express their appreciation of

Mr H. Witt's indefatigable efforts at Changsha in acting as a liaison agent between Mr Becker and the Governor of the Province, who was the representative of the Chinese Government in their efforts to secure the release of the Captives.

To many friends everywhere who have aided by constant believing prayer, and some by personal gifts to cover the various expenses for travelling costs, messengers and escort fees, with other inevitable outlays, our grateful thanks are extended. 'This is the Lord's doing; it is marvellous in our eyes.'

Letter from General Xiao Ke to Alfred Bosshardt

中 华 人 民 共 和 国 驻 英 国 大 使 馆

薄复礼先生：

久违了！从索尔兹伯里先生处知道了你的近况。虽然我们已分别半个世纪，但五十年前你帮我翻译地图事久难忘怀。所以，当索尔兹伯里先生问及此情时，我欣然命笔告之。一九八四年我在出国访问途中，还打听你的下落，以期相晤。如今我们都早过古稀，彼此恐难再见。谨祝健康长寿。

一九八七年五月廿七日于北京

Translation of the letter from General Xiao Ke to Alfred Bosshardt
Embassy of the People's Republic of China

Dear Mr Bosshardt

I haven't heard from you for decades. It was long ago that I heard some latest news about you from Mr Salisbury. Though we have been separated for half-a-century, I still remember very well your generous help in translating the names on some maps for me. When Mr Salisbury mentioned this, I was very pleased to tell him what happened. During my trip abroad in 1984, I tried in vain to contact you. Today we are both well over seventy and I am afraid that it would be very difficult for us to see each other again. I sincerely wish you good health and a long life.

Yours

Xiao Ke

May 27th, 1987, Beijing

Letter from Alfred Bosshardt to General Xiao Ke (edited extracts)

Dear General Xiao Ke

The Embassy of the People's Republic of China in London communicated your friendly greetings by telephone, which gave me much pleasure. This was followed by your kind letter, typed in Chinese characters, which filled my heart with joy. Perhaps by now our mutual friend, Harrison Salisbury, has met you in Beijing and spoken of me. Last year when he was in England he and his good wife visited me. He gave me news of you and spoke highly of you.

I was detained by the Red Army in Guizhou on October 1st, 1934. A few days later you called me to help translate the large detailed map you had acquired which proved so valuable. We were both young then and had both dedicated our lives to bettering mankind, you believing that Communism was the answer and I that the only hope for the world was in Jesus Christ, the Saviour of the world. For your great devotion to the poor and oppressed people and the sacrifices you were making for them, I admired you very much. My memory retains vividly that evening together.

Now half-a-century has passed and we should be wiser men. On January 1st this year I celebrated my ninetieth birthday, glad to be comparatively well and active and happy. I am now more firmly convinced than ever that I have been building on a firm, true foundation. God created the universe and gave to us men the Bible, his word which is truth. He sent us his eternal son, Jesus Christ, to reveal him to mankind. He lived a perfect life on earth and sacrificed that life for man's salvation, to reconcile us to God.

When released on April 12th, at dawn, Easter Sunday, I made my way to Kunming.

Eventually we returned to Guizhou in 1940 and remained there until 1951. For the next fifteen years, my wife and I worked among the overseas Chinese in Laos, and were most happy. Just before we were to retire, my dear wife died at the age of seventy. She is buried in a Chinese cemetery in Laos, but we shall meet again in heaven, where all tears shall be wiped from our eyes.

On hearing that you tried to find me when you passed through Paris, I was deeply touched. I too tried to contact you and sent a letter and my two books by the hand of our mission's general director who was visiting China. He was in Beijing during the great heat and you were absent from the city.

I am sending this via the London Embassy. It comes to you with my very best wishes for good health and a long and active life and much joy. I am thrilled to hear of the progress of China and of the growth of the Chinese Christian church.

With every good wish,

Your sincere friend,

Alfred Bosshardt

August 15th, 1987, Manchester, England

General Xiao Ke's foreword (English translation) to the Chinese edition of *The Guiding Hand*, published in China in 1989*

Mr Alfred Bosshardt's memoirs have now been published in China. Because I was involved in these events and we are old friends, I would like to say a few words, giving background information for those who are unfamiliar with that period of Chinese history.

I first met Mr Bosshardt in early October 1934. At that time I was a general in the Sixth Army of the Red Army. We were marching west through Jiangxi province, and met him accidentally in a small mountain village, the day before we seized Jiuzhou. We had to detain this unknown foreigner, his wife and those travelling with him, because of the tense military situation. The next day we also detained Mr Hayman and his associates whom we met in Jiuzhou.

After some quick investigations, we soon released the family members and associates. But Mr Hayman and Mr Bosshardt were not released. This was because the army had been marching west for more than fifty days and the numbers of sick and injured were increasing daily due to lack of medical supplies. We knew these two missionaries could obtain medical and financial aid for us, so we set this as the condition for their release.

At this time, we were fighting in Guizhou province with only crude maps from school textbooks as our reference. On the second day, in Jiuzhou, we found a map of Guizhou, but the place names were in a foreign language. I sent for Mr Bosshardt because I was told he could

---

*In publishing this foreword by Xiao Ke, the publishers are not thereby endorsing all that the General says here; nor should the fact that a translation of *The Guiding Hand* was published in China lead anyone to assume that Christian books are readily available throughout the country.

speak and read Chinese. This was my first contact with him. At first glance he told me the map was in French. I asked him to help us by translating it, and he spent almost the whole night translating the names into Chinese. As we worked together, I not only gained useful information for the army but I got to know Mr Bosshardt.

At that time I had a bad impression of missionaries. We considered them invaders of our culture so treated them as we treated landlords, confiscating their property and detaining them for ransom. As time passed, I had more contact with Mr Bosshardt. We had many discussions, and jointly organised recreation programmes for the troops. All this brought us to a better understanding. Meanwhile the army had begun to recognise the need for a united front, so my impression of Mr Bosshardt improved. In fact, when he was released on April 12th, 1936, we sent him off with a farewell party as well as enough money for his journey. Altogether he lived with the Red Army for eighteen months. They were memorable months for both of us.

After his release, he went first to Kunming before returning to England. But he could not forget his missionary work in China and returned to resume his work in Guizhou province. After leaving China in 1952, he worked in Laos. His wife died fifteen years later, and he retired to his home town of Manchester in England.

Neither of us expected to re-establish contact after fifty years.

The story of how we managed to get in touch again begins in 1984. When the famous American writer Harrison Salisbury came to China to gather materials for his book, *The Long March – the Untold Story*, he wrote to me enquiring about the missionary who had helped translate the map. Immediately I remembered Mr Bosshardt.

Despite the years between, I can still vividly remember that time, because of the unforgettable military manoeuvre. The maps we had were strategically useless. Mr Bosshardt's expertise in translating the French map came at a very crucial moment and solved a big problem for us. Through his translation he became the army's 'guide' in Guizhou.

As a military commander, I would never forget such help received in time of difficulty, no matter how long ago. So I immediately replied to Mr Salisbury, relating the whole story and asking him to convey my regards to Mr Bosshardt (if he was still living) and his family. After he returned home, Mr Salisbury sent me a copy of Mr Bosshardt's book. Later when he went to England, he located him in Manchester, and they had a long and friendly conversation. Mr Salisbury sent me a photograph of the two of them and a report about their conversation, and conveyed Mr Bosshardt's regards.

I was also able to contact Mr Bosshardt through the Chinese Diplomatic Service. In Autumn 1984 I was on official business in France and, after much searching, I located him early in 1985, through his relative in Switzerland. I received a letter from him through our consulate in France, in which he told me his recent news and sent warm regards. When a British film company came to China, he sent with them a video and two of his books, including this one which is now translated. In May 1987, I wrote to Mr Bosshardt through our diplomatic department. Not long ago, I also sent him a special commemorative magazine for the 60th Anniversary of the People's Liberation Army. I told him how different today's PLA is from the army he had known fifty years ago. He could not come to China to witness the changes for himself, yet I hoped the magazine would give him some idea of them.

That is how we renewed contact after fifty years. I am grateful to Mr Salisbury and to others who helped in making this possible. Their assistance is deeply appreciated.

Some may ask: What is the need for and meaning of this relationship between a missionary and a Communist? I feel such a relationship is both significant and necessary. The revolution in China is victorious now, but the services offered by many foreign friends during the progress towards that victory should be remembered and honoured.

Mr Bosshardt and other missionaries not only brought their

religion to China, but also established schools, translated scientific and technological journals, improved cultural awareness and practised charitable works. All these benefited us. Mr Bosshardt's service to the Red Army was not voluntary but even so he did translate the map and also some English materials; he purchased medical supplies, etc. We had good reason to remember him. I wrote about him in an article in 1980.

In a class-structured society, classes may be antagonistic but the fact that individuals hold differing beliefs need not affect their relationships. In fact they can influence each other and friendship may grow. This is not unusual. History shows that despite differences in points of view or social understanding, there is always a point of common interest or common concern. In the nineteenth century, the humanitarianism of Florence Nightingale and the rapid growth of the Red Cross showed society's common concern to care for the sick and the dying. Mencius, an old Chinese scholar, said, 'Everyone is compassionate.' Indeed, this must be the common concern of all mankind.

This is why peace was the prime concern of most of the world after World War Two. In the past we had a leftist viewpoint: we saw everyone who was not a revolutionary as a counter-revolutionary and vice versa. We absolutely denied any points in common with other countries, classes and social groups. We had lost the ability to look for things in common or how to use a common language to exchange points of view and come to agreement. This was a great loss to us. Now mankind's prime concern is to establish a peaceful international environment. So we need more international friends to get to know China, to understand China and eventually to help China. Then China can fully utilise the power of unity.

Although we detained Mr Bosshardt, he held no grudges against us. We should admire his heart and attitude and value our contact with him.

Let us now talk about Mr Bosshardt's book. *The Guiding Hand*, his second book, was written in 1974. Since he was a missionary, he wrote to 'propaganda' God. The title refers to God, meaning that God was guiding him. In his foreword he attributed his survival to God's mercy. Obviously we differ on this point because we are Marxist atheists. So what do we appreciate in his book?

Some say that he as a foreigner objectively reported the Long March. As his first book, *The Restraining Hand*, was published in 1936, his account was a year earlier than that of Mr Edgar Snow in his book *Red Star Over China*.*

Others said that he refuted the official and media allegations that those in the Red Army were bandits and pirates. At that time, Chiang Kai-shek and the pro-China Westerners were constantly referring to the Red Army as bandits. On the other hand, Mr Bosshardt says, 'These people were actually firm believers in Communism, Marxism and Leninism and they practised the principles.' He did not consider them bandits or pirates.

I consider the most important aspect however to be his angle on the history of the Red Army. There are many aspects to history. For a time we only looked at one aspect, and refused to consider other angles, especially negative ones. During the Period of Unrest this was particularly true; many books were forbidden and could not be published. I felt this was not good.

Mr Bosshardt viewed the Red Army from the point of view of a missionary, and tried to understand it. He recorded all his observations and feelings. This is truly of historical value and will be of great use to us as we study the Red Army.

Of course when studying history one must have one's own viewpoint and method, not just parrot the views of others or lose perspective. Some points in Mr Bosshardt's book were not quite accurate. For example, he attributed his release to God. In fact it was because of the gradual improvement in our thought policy. In the past we did some foolish things. Despite our policy of giving preferential treatment to prisoners of war, we eliminated high-level

---

*Published in London in 1937.

officers such as the celebrated Zhan Huizhan.* But following developments and changes in the world and in China, and the encroachment of Japanese imperialism, our understanding changed. So we no longer killed that sort of person. Mr Bosshardt mentions in the book† how we asked Lieutenant-General Zhang‡ of the Kuomintang to be a tactics instructor at the Red Army school. He also mentions Zhou Suyuan,§ a high-ranking official with us on the Long March, who set up the resistance against Japan in north-western Guizhou.

What caused the change? At that time we were under Communist International direction for an anti-fascist united front, and the central committee's policy of opposing Japan and opposing Chiang Kai-shek. As we began to understand the need to gain others' support for this united front, especially after the central committee's declaration of August 1st, we became more conscious of our behaviour, and our manner towards Mr Bosshardt gradually changed. When we were outside Kunming, we released him unconditionally. So when reading this book, it is necessary to pay attention to the historical background and to have an analytical mind.

What is the way to study history? In the early 1970s I met two comrades who were arguing about where Mao Zedong would send regiment leader Lin Biao.** Each insisted that he was correct and they continued to argue. Others discussed Lin Biao before he plunged to his death, saying he was involved in uprisings. After his

---

*A Nationalist general who was captured and publicly humiliated and then beheaded by the Communists.

†*The Restraining Hand*, Hodder & Stoughton 1936.

‡General Zhang Zhenhan, Nationalist commander, captured in early summer 1935 by General Xiao Ke.

§Former governor of Guizhou and a scholar, who helped He Long at Bijie during the Long March.

**Defence Minister, who died in mysterious circumstances, the official version being that he was killed in a plane crash in 1971 whilst flying to Moscow after trying to murder Mao Zedong. Without clearing up the mystery, Xiao Ke drops a few disapproving hints concerning what was going on at the time.

death he lost his rank amid all the gossip and hearsay. This is not good. History is history and cannot be unilaterally distorted to serve politics. There is only one truth which cannot be altered just to suit the needs of politics.

When discussing historical problems, some amplify good points while others dwell on the bad points or take to fabrication. Another person quotes the sayings of those in authority or of famous people. But historical facts are the best authority, so one must stick to the facts and be truthful when studying history. In order to clarify all the facts, it is important to make a thorough search for all previous records, including both complimentary and critical materials. Compliments may not be constructive while criticisms may not be altogether destructive. It all depends how we deal with them.

We did make some mistakes after the set up of the Communist Party. We do not want to talk about them, but it is not right to prevent others from doing so. Those who criticise may have their own standpoints and we must see whether this is the truth.

In his book Mr Bosshardt could not praise us, but as long as it is a historical account, it could be of historical value. It will not harm those already dead to reveal past mistakes, and could be educational in the present.

To conclude, in the process of studying history the first step must be to sort out the facts, to thoroughly research all previous historical records. The facts should be evaluated and all connections established. Through analysis to conclusion, the progress of history will be revealed. The principle of studying history is to pursue the truth, and this is one of the reasons for publishing books like this one.

Alfred Bosshardt's foreword to the Chinese edition of
The Guiding Hand, **published in China in 1989**

It was certainly an honour to be invited by General Xiao Ke to write a foreword to the Chinese edition of my book *The Guiding Hand*.

To be reinstated as an 'old friend of the Chinese people' has been one of the joys of my old age. And it is an added joy to hear of the translation of my book.

As I type these few lines, seated at my desk in Manchester, England, I can see an enlarged photograph in colour of Xiao Ke as he is today at the age of eighty. He is also seated at his desk writing a few lines for me in the magnificent, well-illustrated book he sent as a present for me.

It is over fifty years since I last saw him on the eve of my release from eighteen months' imprisonment with the Red Army. That was on Easter Day at dawn, April 12th, 1936. My wife and I were captured by his men on October 1st, 1934. For the next month we marched onward without pause. Three times we walked all day, all night and all day again the next day.

Early in that month, after a tiring march, the General called for me one evening to help him decipher a detailed map of Guizhou province that had just fallen into the Red Army's hands. This was my first view of the General. He was then twenty-five years of age, with a fine military physique and a genial disposition. It was soon obvious to me that he was a cultured, educated man and born leader. I could not but admire him, though we came from such different backgrounds. Why, I wondered, did this man, who could have enjoyed a life of ease and pleasure, throw in his lot with those who were striving to bring justice to the poor, oppressed peasants who made up eighty per cent of China's population? It meant for him dire hardship and real danger to life. His relations and friends were also, no doubt, mystified by his actions. But in his teens he had read the writings of Marx and Lenin and accepted their ideology, confident that it could solve China's problems.

I, too, had been won over in my early life – but by the revolutionary teachings of Jesus Christ. Through the Holy Bible, the inspired word of God – creator of heaven and earth – which also contains the history and doctrine of Jesus, I dedicated my life to work for the uplift of mankind.

Christ is revealed plainly in the Bible. He was from the beginning, even before the creation, the eternal and only son of God. Two thousand years ago, at the command of his Father, he gave up the glories of heaven to come to this sinful earth, born of a virgin into a poor working-class family. He lived a sinless life, went about preaching, healing the sick and performing many other miracles. 'But such a cruel death he died: he was hung up and crucified; and those kind hands which did such good – they nailed them to a cross of wood.' He is the only person who could have merited heaven by his perfect life, but he freely laid it down and shed his life-blood to bear the punishment of God for our rebellion against our maker. In other words, he died for our sin and offences. God received this sacrifice of his son and showed it by raising him up on the third day after his burial. His disciples saw him alive during forty days: 500 of them at one time. Then he ascended into heaven to be our advocate with God. His last command to his disciples was: 'Go into all the world and preach my good news to everyone. All believers will not perish but have eternal life after death.'

When I was only ten years of age, I heard God calling me to go to China. So in 1922, after two years of special training for work in China, I left home and friends behind. Eventually I found myself in Guizhou, one of China's poorest provinces. Few foreigners resided there and I was isolated from other European folk. The work was hard, for there were no roads that would take wheeled vehicles, and that very often meant travelling long distances on foot. Also there was constant unrest from widespread brigandage. But despite these dangers and adverse circumstances, I was tremendously happy. Why? Because I had the assurance that I was where God would have me be, and doing what he would have me do. My motives for being in China were pure. God had given me a special love for the Chinese people.

While a prisoner with the Red Army, I still knew that God had allowed it for some good purpose – and that made all the difference. It was very hard to be cursed and judged to be a spy for the Imperialists, and thus an enemy of the people, worthy of capital punishment. But the whole eighteen months of hardship and suffering was a wonderful spiritual experience and I proved, as I could not otherwise have done, that when stripped of all luxuries and many needs, I had the comfort of God's promise never to leave me nor forsake me. During the gravest dangers and worst trials, I experienced more than ever before his help, his strength and his comfort. Without this, I do not think I would have come through alive. So I thank God for this experience.

Now more than fifty years have passed, and I am more sure than ever that I have been building my life on a true foundation. After release, on arrival at Kunming in Yunnan province, the doctor who examined me told me I could not have lived another ten days. After five months of good nursing, the doctors told me not to expect a long life. My body, they said, had been so weakened by disease that my life would be cut short by at least ten years. But now at ninety-one years of age I am still well and happy – and still of some use. Thus I am a witness to his power to heal and strengthen. The peace of heart he gives me passes all understanding.

So I commend to you this which is a simple story of part of my life. I trust you may be helped by it to become better and more useful citizens of your great country. I receive many accounts of the progress of your land and rejoice for all the improvements. I am truly glad that after much suffering you are experiencing a better and richer life. I pray daily for all who are in responsible positions in the government, in schools and colleges and in homes. And I trust that each one of you may learn to forget your own pleasures and find satisfaction in respecting and loving one another. Peace be with you!

R. Alfred Bosshardt

Messages of condolence from Chinese officials to Alfred Bosshardt's relatives

From Fu Zhiwei, Embassy of the People's Republic of China

I was shocked to learn the sad news from Mr Anthony Grey that Alfred had passed away. I sent the news to General Xiao Ke soon after I got the news. I enclose herewith his letter to the family of Mr Alfred Bosshardt which he faxed me today.

I am so sorry that Alfred could not see the film about his story during the Long March. But we'll keep trying to produce it successfully to his memory.

From Ji Chaozhu, Under-Secretary-General, Department for Development Support and Management Services, Beijing

I was very much saddened to learn of the passing of my friend Mr Alfred Bosshardt, who was always a dear friend of the Chinese people and who did so much to promote better relations between China and the United Kingdom. Please extend my deep condolences to Mr Bosshardt's family. He will always remain in my heart. Let us all remember him as an inspiration to us in our work for world peace and understanding and friendship among peoples.

From Ma Yuzhen, Ambassador, Embassy of the People's Republic of China

Shocked to learn of the sad news of the passing away of Mr Alfred Bosshardt, I wish to express my sincere condolences. Mr Bosshardt did a great deal for the promotion of understanding and relations between the people of our two countries. He will always be remembered as an old friend of the Chinese people.

From Xiao Ke, the general who held Alfred captive during the Long March

薄复礼亲属：

　　惊悉薄复礼先生仙逝，谨向这位长征时期的同道朋友表示哀悼。

[signature]

一九九三年十二月十六日

Translation:
Concerning Bo Fu-li (Alfred Bosshardt)
I send my sincere condolences on the death of Mr Alfred Bosshardt, as I respectfully remember this fellow-traveller and friend of the Long March and send my deep sympathy.

Xiao Ke

December 16th, 1993

English Speaking OMF Centres

OMF
PO Box 849
Epping
NSW 2121
AUSTRALIA

OMF
PO Box 10-159
Balmoral
Auckland 1
NEW ZEALAND

OMF
5759 Coopers Avenue
Mississauga ON
L4Z 1R9
CANADA

OMF
10 West Dry Creek Circle
Littleton
CO 80120-4413
USA

OMF
2 Cluny Road
Singapore 1025
REPUBLIC OF SINGAPORE

OMF
PO Box 53041
Kenilworth 7745
SOUTH AFRICA

HUDSON TAYLOR:
LESSONS IN DISCIPLESHIP

by Roger Steer (Author of *A Man in Christ*)

Hudson Taylor (1832-1905) was one of the most remarkable missionaries the UK has ever produced. Although he was unremarkable in appearance, Taylor's quiet yet passionate manner inspired hundreds of men and women to go to China as missionaries and many others to pray for its 'lost millions'. Taylor founded the China Inland Mission in 1865 and now as OMF International, it has around a thousand workers spread across East Asia.

Roger Steer, Taylor's biographer, has drawn one hundred lessons from his life and writings on themes such as holiness, prayer, knowing God and the way of the Cross, and combines fascinating biographical detail with very strong spiritual content. 'As I have reflected on Hudson Taylor's life, I have grown convinced that the insights of this man of prayer, profound thought and action come close to capturing the essence of Christianity'.

Co-published with OMF International

ISBN 1 85424 332 5   160pp large format   £5.99

ORDER FORM

Please send me:

____ copies of HUDSON TAYLOR:
LESSONS IN DISCIPLESHIP   @ £5.99 _____
Postage and packing 80p
(orders above £10.00 post free in UK)   _____

TOTAL £ _____

Name (Dr/Rev/Mr/Mrs/Miss/Ms) _____

_____

Address _____

_____ Postcode _____

☐ I enclose a cheque for £____ (payable to Monarch Publications)

or

☐ please debit my credit card £____

Mastercard (inc Access and Eurocard)/Visa

Credit card number

Card expiry date _____

Signature of cardholder _____

Cardholder's name and initials
(as shown on card) _____

*Please return to: Monarch Publications, Broadway House, The Broadway,
Crowborough, East Sussex TN6 1HQ.
(Tel: 01892 652364 Fax: 01892 663329)*